Express.js Deep API Reference

Azat Mardan

Apress®

Managing Director: Welmoed Spahr
Lead Editor: Ben Renow-Clarke
Technical Reviewer: Peter Elst
Editorial Board: Steve Anglin, Mark Beckner, Ewan Buckingham, Gary Cornell, Louise Corrigan, Jim DeWolf, Jonathan Gennick, Robert Hutchinson, Michelle Lowman, James Markham, Matthew Moodie, Jeff Olson, Jeffrey Pepper, Douglas Pundick, Ben Renow-Clarke, Dominic Shakeshaft, Gwenan Spearing, Matt Wade, Steve Weiss
Coordinating Editor: Christine Ricketts
Copy Editor: William McManus
Compositor: SPi Global
Indexer: SPi Global
Artist: SPi Global
Cover Designer: Anna Ishchenko

Distributed to the book trade worldwide by Springer Science+Business Media New York, 233 Spring Street, 6th Floor, New York, NY 10013. Phone 1-800-SPRINGER, fax (201) 348-4505, e-mail orders-ny@springer-sbm.com, or visit www.springeronline.com. Apress Media, LLC is a California LLC and the sole member (owner) is Springer Science + Business Media Finance Inc (SSBM Finance Inc). SSBM Finance Inc is a Delaware corporation.

For information on translations, please e-mail rights@apress.com, or visit www.apress.com.

Apress and friends of ED books may be purchased in bulk for academic, corporate, or promotional use. eBook versions and licenses are also available for most titles. For more information, reference our Special Bulk Sales–eBook Licensing web page at www.apress.com/bulk-sales.

Any source code or other supplementary material referenced by the author in this text is available to readers at www.apress.com. For detailed information about how to locate your book's source code, go to www.apress.com/source-code/.

Contents at a Glance

Contents

About the Author

Azat Mardan has over a dozen years of experience in web, mobile, and software engineering. With a Bachelor of Science in Informatics and a Master of Science in Information Systems Technology, Azat possesses deep academic knowledge as well as extensive practical experience. He is the author of eight other books on JavaScript and Node.js, including Practical Node.js (Apress, 2014), and Rapid Prototyping with JS, an Amazon.com #1 Best Seller in its category.

Currently, Azat teaches the Node Program (http://nodeprogram.com) and creates online courses, while also working as a Team Lead at DocuSign.com. His team rebuilds a 50 million user product (DocuSign web app) using the cutting-edge tech stack of Node.js, Express.js, Backbone.js, CoffeeScript, Jade, Stylus, and Redis.

Recently, Azat worked as an engineer at the curated social media news aggregator web site Storify.com (acquired by LiveFyre.com in 2013), which is used by BBC, NBC, CNN, The White House, and others. Storify is a partner of Joyent.com (Node.js maintainer) and runs completely on Node.js, (whereas most companies that use Node.js use it only for certain tasks). Storify.com is the company behind the open source library jade-browser.

Prior to his stint at Storify.com, Azat developed mission-critical applications for government agencies in Washington, DC, including the National Institutes of Health, the National Center for Biotechnology Information, and the Federal Deposit Insurance Corporation, as well as for Lockheed Martin.

Azat has received acclaim for teaching programming classes at Marakana (acquired by Twitter in 2013), pariSOMA, General Assembly San Francisco, and Hack Reactor. In his spare time, Azat writes about technology on his blog http://webapplog.com.

Azat is the creator of several open source Node.js projects, including ExpressWorks, mongoui, HackHall.com, and NodeFramework.com, and is a contributor to express, oauth, jade-browser, and other NPM modules.

About the Technical Reviewer

Peter Elst is a web standards enthusiast coming from a multimedia and application development background and works as a Web Solutions Engineer in Creative Innovation at Google.

With well over a decade experience, Peter is a regular technical reviewer, co-authored a number of books including "HTML5 Solutions - Essential Techniques for HTML5 Developers" and is a well respected speaker at many industry events. You can find out more about his latest interests and ongoing projects on his personal blog peterelst.com.

Acknowledgments

This book would not be possible without the existence of my parents, the Internet and JavaScript. Furthermore, I acknowledge the geniuses of Ryan Dahl (Node.js) and TJ Holowaychuk (Express.js).

I express my gratitude to Apress editors who persuaded me to continue with publishing this book as a remake of Express.js Guide, and who have put a lot of energy into making the book great: Christine Ricketts, Peter Elst, and William McManus. Also special thanks to Tom Rutka.

Last but not least, I would like to thank my high school teacher who always had many toy problems for us to solve using Turbo Pascal.

Introduction

Please read this Introduction carefully to avoid any confusion. Read it especially if you are considering buying this book to make sure it perfectly suits your level of expertise and needs. If you bought Express.js Deep API Reference already, then congratulations! As a reader of this book you are in a great position to dig deeper into the most popular web framework for the fastest growing platform.

The demand for the skills in these technologies grows along with both categories of employers (startups and big corporations) adopting Node.js. The reason for that is that there's always a gap between early adopters and mainstream ones. We are rapidly approaching the mainstream (it's 2014-2015 during this writing). The earlier you, as a developer, jump on Node.js, the better, because if you aren't growing, you are dying.

In this Introduction, I'll cover the following topics that will help you to get the most of the book:

Why This Book Was Written

Experss.js Deep API Reference is a derivative work from Pro Express.js. This means that this book is a more focused and concise manual for the Express.js framework. But this book has started as Express.js Guide a few years ago.

The Express.js Guide (2013) was on of the first books on Express.js, which is the most popular Node.js web framework yet (as of this writing, December of 2014). That book was one of the first solely dedicated to the framework. Back in the day, Express.js' official website (expressjs.com) had only bits of insights, and those were for advanced Node.js programmers. So no wonder that I've found that many people — including those who go through the HackReactor8 program and come to my Node.js classes at General Assembly and pariSOMA — were interested in a definitive manual; one that would cover how all the different components of Express.js work together in real life. The goal of The Express.js Guide was to be that resource.

After the Express.js Guide became the Amazon.com #1 Best Seller in its category, Apress approached me to write this book. Express.js Deep API Reference is much more than a revision or an update of Express.js Guide. It's a complete remake, because this book includes more things like: comments, descriptions, examples, and extras. The new book also has better-reviewed code and text, and up-to-date versions of the libraries (e.g., Express.js v4.8.1).

Many things have changed between writing the two books. Node.js was forked at io.js. TJ Holowaychuk, the creator of Express.js, stopped being actively involved with Node.js and StrongLoop maintains the framework's repository. The development on Express.js is as rapid as ever. It's more stable and more secure. And I see nothing but a brighter future for Express.js and Node.js!

Who Should Own This Book

This book is intended for software engineers and web developers already fluent in programming and front-end JavaScript. To get the most of the benefits of Express.js Deep API Reference, readers must be familiar with basic Node.js concepts, like process and global, and know core modules, including stream, cluster, and buffer.

If you're thinking about starting a Node.js project or about rewriting an existing one, and your weapon of choice is Express.js — this guide is for you! It will answer most of your "how" and "why" questions.

What This Book Is

Express.js Deep API Reference is a concise book on one particular library. Unlike Practical Node.js (Apress, 2014) which covered many libraries, Express.js Deep API Reference is focused only on the single module — Express.js. Of course, in places where it's necessary to cover other related libraries, like middleware, the book touches on those as well, but not as extensively as on the framework itself.

Express.js Deep API Reference covers configuration, settings, middleware, rendering templates, request and response objects, routing, extracting params from dynamic URLs, and error handling.

There are seven chapters in Express.js Deep API Reference:

1. Configuration, Settings and Environments

2. Working with Middleware

3. Template Engines and Consolidate.js

4. Parameters and Routing

5. Request

6. Response

7. Error Handling and Running an App

For more details on what the book covers, please refer to the Table of Contents.

What This Book is Not

This book is not an introduction to Node.js, nor is it a book that covers all aspects of building a modern-day web application in great details, e.g., websockets, databases, and (of course) front-end development. Also, keep in mind that readers won't find in Express.js Deep API Reference aids for learning programming and/or JavaScript fundamentals here, because this is not a beginners' book.

For an introduction to Node.js, MongoDB, and front-end development with Backbone.js, you might want to take a look at Azat's book, Rapid Prototyping with JS: Agile JavaScript Development10, and the Node Program (nodeprogram.com) in person and online courses.

In the real world, and especially in Node.js development, due to its modularized philosophy, we seldom use just a single framework. In this book, we have tried to stick to Express.js and leave everything else out as much as possible, without compromising the usefulness of the examples. Therefore, we intentionally left out some important chunks of web development — for example, databases, authentication and testing. Although these elements are present in tutorials and examples, they're not explained in detail. For those materials, you could take a look at the books in the Appendix A: Related Reading and Resources at the end of this book.

Examples

The Express.js Deep API Reference book is full of code snippets and run-ready examples. Most of them are abridged code examples that serve the purpose of illustrating a particular point.

The bulk of the source code is available in the GitHub repository at github.com/ azat-co/expressapiref under ch1-ch7 (for chapters 1 to 7).

The provided examples were written and tested only with the given, specific versions of dependencies. Because Node.js and its ecosystem of modules are being developed rapidly, please pay attention to whether new versions have breaking changes. Here is the list of versions that we've used:

```
Express.js v4.8.1

Node.js v0.10.12

NPM v1.2.32

MongoDB v2.6.3

Redis v2.6.7

Stylus v0.47.3

Jade v1.5.0

Foreman v0.75.0

Google Chrome Version 39.0.2171.7
```

Errata and Contacts

If you get stuck on an exercise, make sure to check the GitHub repository. It might have more recent code and answers in the GitHub Issues section. Also, by submitting your issues you can help the experience better for you fellow programmers: http://github.com/azat-co/expressapiref/issues.

As for the pesky typos, which I'm sure will still remain no matter how many times we edited the manuscript, submit them to Apress or GitHub Issues.

Finally, let's be friends on the Internet! It's lonely to code in isolation. Here are some of the ways to reach the author:

- Write an Amazon.com review: `http://amzn.to/1vVVKCR`

- Join HackHall.com: community for programmers, hackers, and developers

- Tweet Node.js question on Twitter: `@azat_co`

- Follow Azat on Facebook: `facebook.com/164048499437`

- Visit the Express.js Deep API Reference website: `http:// expressapiref.com`

- Visit the Azat's website: `http://azat.co`

- Star Express.js Deep API Reference GitHub repository: `github.com/azat-co/expressapiref`

- Email Azat directly: `hi@azat.co`

- Sign up for the blog's newsletter: `webapplog.com`

It's the end of the Introduction. Thank you for reading it. You can share that you're about to start learning Express.js on Twitter by clicking on this link: `http://ctt.ec/09Sc5`.

■ ■ ■

CHAPTER 1

Configuration, Settings, and Environments

This chapter is all about different ways of configuring Express.js settings. As you might have heard, Express.js positions itself as a *configuration over convention* framework. So, when it comes to configurations in Express.js, you can configure pretty much anything! To do so, you use configuration statements and know the settings.

What are the settings? Think of settings as key-value pairs that typically act in a global or application-wide manner. Settings can augment behavior of the server, add information to responses, or be used for references later.

There are two types of settings: Express.js system settings that the framework uses behind the scene, and arbitrary settings that developers use for their own code. The former come with default values so that if you don't configure them—the app will still run okay! Therefore, it's not a big deal if you don't know or don't use some of the Express.js settings. For this reason, don't feel like you must learn all the settings by heart to be able to build Express apps. Just use this chapter as a reference any time you have a question about a specific method or a system setting.

To progress from simple to more complex things, this chapter is organized as follows:

- *Configuration*: Methods to set settings values and to get them

- *Settings*: Names of the settings, their default values, what they affect, and examples of how to augment values

- *Environments*: Determining an environment and putting an application in that mode is an important aspect of any serious application.

The examples for this chapter are available in the ch1/app.js project, which is in the GitHub repository at http://github.com/azat-co/proexpressjs.

Configuration

Before you can work with settings, you need to learn how to apply them on an Express.js app. The most common and versatile way is to use app.set to define a value and use app.get to retrieve the value based on the key/name of the setting.

The other configuration methods are less versatile, because they apply only to certain settings based on their type (boolean): `app.enable()` and `app.disable()`.

app.set() and app.get()

The method `app.set(name, value)` accepts two parameters: `name` and `value`. As you might guess, it sets the value for the name. For example, we often want to store the value of the port on which we plan to start our server:

```
app.set('port', 3000);
```

Or, for a more advanced and realistic use case, we can grab the port from system environment variable `PORT` (`process.env.PORT`). If the `PORT` environment variable is undefined, we fall back to the hard-coded value 3000:

```
app.set('port', process.env.PORT || 3000);
```

The preceding code is a shorter equivalent to using an `if else` statement:

```
if (process.env.PORT) {
  app.set(process.env.PORT);
} else {
  app.set(3000);
}
```

The name value could be an Express.js setting or an arbitrary string. To get the value, we can use `app.set(name)` with a single parameter, or we can use the more explicit method `app.get(name)`, as shown in the following example:

```
console.log('Express server listening on port ' + app.get('port'));
```

The `app.set()` method also exposes variables to templates application-wide; for example,

```
app.set('appName', 'HackHall');
```

will be available in *all* templates, meaning this example would be valid in a Jade template layout:

```
doctype 5
html
  head
    title= appName
  body
    block content
```

app.enable() and app.disable()

There are some system Express.js settings that have the type of boolean true and false, instead of the string type, and they can only be set to boolean false or true. For such flags, there are shorthand versions; for example, as an alternative to the app.set(name, true) and app.set(name, false) functions, you can use the concise app.enable(name) and app.disable(name) calls accordingly. I recommend using app.set() because it keeps the code consistent no matter what is the type of the setting.

For example, the etag Express.js setting is a boolean. It turns ETag headers on and off for browser caching (more on etag later). To turn this caching off with app.disable() write a statement:

```
app.disable('etag');
```

app.enabled() and app.disabled()

To check whether the aforementioned values equal true or false, we can call methods app.enabled(name) and app.disabled(name). For example,

```
app.disable('etag');
console.log(app.disabled('etag'));
```

will output true in the context of the Express.js app.

Settings

There are two categories of settings:

- *Express.js system settings*: These settings are used by the framework to determine certain configurations. Most of them have default values, so the bare-bones app that omits configuring these settings will work just fine.

- *Custom settings*: You can store any arbitrary name as a setting for reference later. These settings are custom to your application, and you first need to define them to use.

Coverage of system settings is one of the most obscure parts of Express.js documentation, because some of the settings are not documented at all (as of this writing). Express.js is flexible enough so that you don't have to know **all the settings** in order to write apps. But after you've learned about all the setting and have begun to use the ones that you need, you will be more confident in configuring your server. You'll understand the inner workings of the framework better.

In this section, you'll learn about the following settings:

- env
- view cache
- view engine
- views
- trust proxy
- jsonp callback name
- json replacer and json spaces
- case sensitive routing
- strict routing
- x-powered-by
- etag
- query parser
- subdomain offset

To illustrate settings in action, we wrote a ch1/app.js example. To avoid confusion, we'll refrain from showing the whole file now, and instead provide the source code at the end of this section for reference.

env

This variable is used to store the current environment mode for this particular Node.js process. The value is automatically set by Express.js from process.env.NODE_ENV (which is fed to Node.js through an environment variable on the executing machine) or, if that is not set, to the development value.

The other most common values for env setting are as follows:

- development
- test
- stage
- preview
- production

The "production" and "development" values are used by Express.js for certain settings' defaults (view cache is one of them). The other values are just convention, meaning you're free to use whatever you want, as long as you are consistent. For example, instead of stage you can use qa.

We can augment the env setting by adding app.set('env', 'preview'); or process.env.NODE_ENV=preview in our code. However, the better way is to start an app with $ NODE_ENV=preview node app or to set the NODE_ENV variable on the machine.

Knowing in what mode the application runs is very important because logic related to error handling, compilation of style sheets, and rendering of the templates can differ dramatically. Obviously, databases and hostnames are different from environment to environment.

The app.get('env') setting is illustrated in the ch1/app.js example as

```
console.log(app.get('env'));
```

This line outputs

```
"development"
```

The preceding line is printed if NODE_ENV is set to development when we launch the process with $ NODE_ENV=development node app.js or when NODE_ENV is not set. In the latter case, the reason for the "development" value is that Express.js defaults the setting to "development" when it's undefined.

view cache

This flag, if set to false, allows for painless development because templates are read each time the server requests them. On the other hand, if view cache is set to true, it facilitates template compilation caching, which is a desired behavior in production. If the env setting is production, then view cache is enabled by default. Otherwise it is set to false.

view engine

The view engine setting holds the template file extension (e.g., 'ext' or 'jade') to utilize if the file extension is not passed to the res.render() function inside of the request handler.

For example, as shown in Figure 1-1, if we comment out the line from the cli-app/app.js example:

```
// app.set('view engine', 'ejs');
```

The server won't be able to locate the file because our instructions in cli-app/routes/index.js are too ambiguous:

```
exports.index = function(req, res){
  res.render('index', { title: 'Express' });
};
```

5

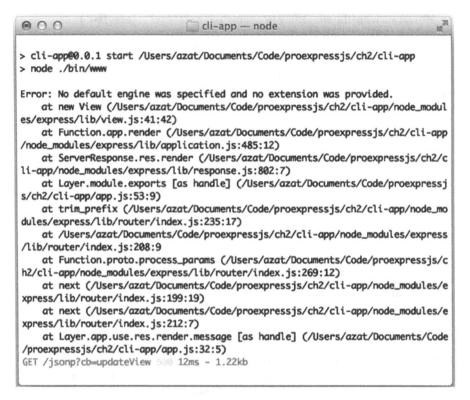

Figure 1-1. *The result of not having a proper template extension set*

We can fix this by adding an extension to the cli-app/routes/index.js file:

```
exports.index = function(req, res){
  res.render('index.ejs', { title: 'Express' });
};
```

For more information on how to apply different template engines, please refer to the Chapter 3.

views

The views setting has an absolute path (starts with / on Mac and Unix) to a directory with templates. This setting defaults to the absolute path of the views folder in the project's root (where the main application file, e.g., app.js, is).

In Express.js, changing the template folder name is trivial. Typically, when we set the custom value for views in app.js, we use path.join() and the __dirname global variable—which gives us the absolute path to the folder where app.js is. For example, if you want to use folder templates use this configuration statement:

```
app.set('views', path.join(__dirname, 'templates'));
```

trust proxy

Set trust proxy to true if your Node.js app is working behind reverse proxy such as Varnish or Nginx. This will permit trusting in the X-Forwarded-* headers, such as X-Forwarded-Proto (req.protocol) or X-Forwarder-For (req.ips). The trust proxy setting is disabled by default.

If you want to turn it on (when you have a proxy server) you can use one of these statements:

```
app.set('trust proxy', true);
app.enable('trust proxy');
```

jsonp callback name

If you're building an application (a REST API server) that serves requests coming from front-end clients hosted on different domains, you might encounter cross-domain limitations when making XHR/AJAX calls. In other words, browser requests are limited to the same domain (and port). The workaround is to use cross-origin resource sharing (CORS) headers on the server.

If you don't want to apply CORS headers to your server, then the JavaScript object literal notation with prefix (JSONP) is the way to go. Express.js has a res.jsonp() method that makes using JSONP a breeze.

■ **Tip**   To find out more about CORS, go to http://en.wikipedia.org/wiki/Cross-origin_resource_sharing.

The default callback name, which is a prefix for our JSONP response, is usually provided in the query string of the request with the name callback; for example, ?callback=updateView. However, if you want to use something different, just set the setting jsonp callback name to that value; for example, for the requests with a query string param ?cb=updateView, we can use this setting:

```
app.set('jsonp callback name', 'cb');
```

That way, our responses would be wrapped in updateView JavaScript code (with the proper Content-Type header, of course) as shown in Figure 1-2.

Figure 1-2. Using cb as the query string name for the callback

In most cases, we don't want to alter this value because the default callback value is somewhat standardized by jQuery $.ajax JSONP functions.

If we set jsonp callback name to cb in the Express.js setting configuration, but make a request with a different property, such as callback, then the route won't output JSONP. It will default to JSON format, as shown in Figure 1-3, without the prefix of the function call, which we saw in Figure 1-2.

Figure 1-3. *Without the proper callback parameter, JSONP defaults to JSON*

json replacer and json spaces

Likewise, when we use the Express.js method res.json(), we can apply special parameters: replacer and spaces. These parameters are passed to all JSON.stringify() functions[1] in the scope of the application. JSON.stringify() is a widely used function for transforming native JavaScript/Node.js objects into strings.

The replacer parameter acts like a filter. It's a function that takes two arguments: key and value. If undefined is returned, then the value is omitted. For the key-value pair to make it to the final string, we need to return the value. You can read more about replacer at Mozilla Developer Network (MDN).[2]

Express.js uses null as the default value for json replacer. I often use JSON.stringify(obj, null, 2) when I need to print pretty JSON.

The spaces parameter is in essence an indentation size. Its value defaults to 2 in development and to 0 in production. In most cases, we leave these settings alone.

---

[1]https://developer.mozilla.org/en-US/docs/Web/JavaScript/Reference/Global_Objects/JSON/stringify
[2]https://developer.mozilla.org/en-US/docs/Using_native_JSON#The_replacer_parameter

In our example app ch1/app.js, we have a /json route that sends us back an object with a book's information. We define a replacer parameter as a function that omits the discount code from the object (we don't want to expose this info). And the spaces parameter is set to 4 so that we can see JSON that is nicely formatted for humans instead of some jumbled code. The resulting response for the /json route is shown in Figure 1-4.

Figure 1-4. *JSON output with replacer and spaces set*

These are the statements used in the example app:

```
app.set('json replacer', function(key, value){
  if (key === 'discount')
    return undefined;
  else
    return value;
});
app.set('json spaces', 4);
```

If we remove json spaces, the app will produce the results shown in Figure 1-5.

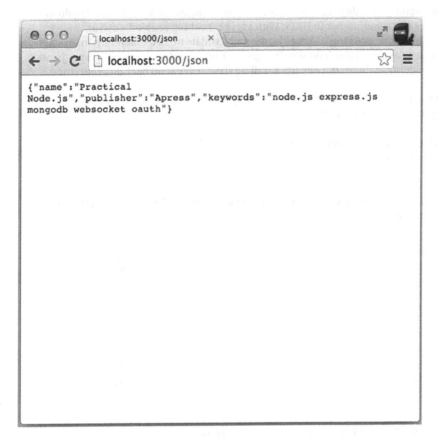

Figure 1-5. *JSON output without spaces set*

case sensitive routing

The case sensitive routing flag should be self-explanatory. We disregard the case of the URL paths when it's false, which is the default value, and do otherwise when the value is set to true. For example, if we have app.enable('case sensitive routing');, then /users and /Users won't be the same. It's best to have this option disabled for the sake of avoiding confusion.

strict routing

The next setting (or a flag because it has the boolean meaning) strict routing deals with cases of trailing slashes in URLs. With strict routing enabled, such as app.set('strict routing', true');, the paths will be treated differently; for example, /users and /users/ will be completely separate routes. In the example ch1/app.js, we have two identical routes but one has a trailing slash. They send back different strings:

```
app.get('/users', function(request, response){
  response.send('users');
})
app.get('/users/', function(request, response){
  response.send('users/');
})
```

As a result, the browser will have different messages for /users and /users/, as shown in Figure 1-6.

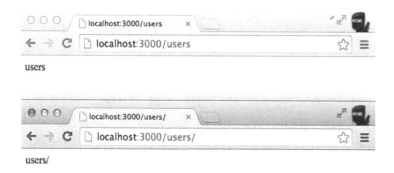

Figure 1-6. *With strict routing enabled, /users and users/ are different routes*

By default, this parameter is set to false, which means that the trailing slash is ignored and those routes with a trailing slash will be treated the same as their counterparts without a trailing slash. My recommendation is to leave the default value; that is, treat the routes with slashes the same as the routes without slashes. This recommendation doesn't apply if your API architecture requires them to be treated differently.

x-powered-by

The x-powered-by option sets the HTTP response header X-Powered-By to the Express value. This option is enabled by default, as you can see in Figure 1-7.

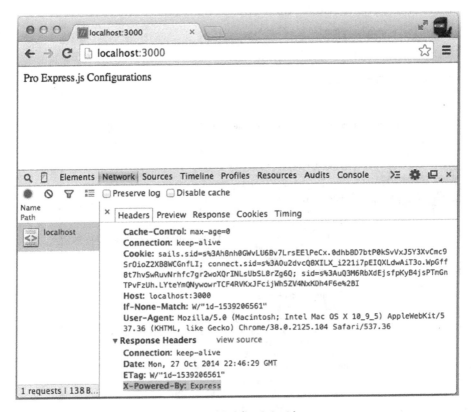

Figure 1-7. *X-Powered-By Express is enabled (by default)*

If you want to disable x-powered-by (remove it from the response)—which is recommended for security reasons, because it's harder to find vulnerabilities if your platform is unknown—then apply app.set('x-powered-by', false) or app.disable('x-powered-by'), which removes the X-Powered-By response header (as in the example ch1/app.js and as shown in Figure 1-8).

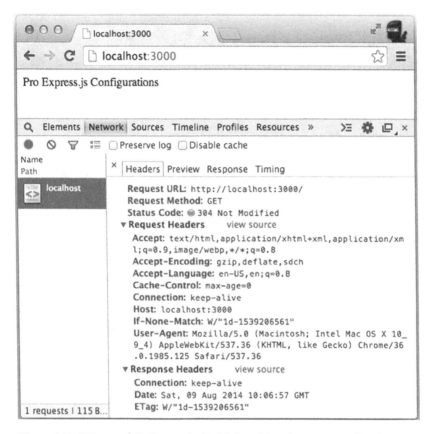

Figure 1-8. *X-Powered-By Express is disabled and there's no response header*

etag

ETag[3] (or entity tag) is a caching tool. The way it works is akin to the unique identifier for the content on a given URL. In other words, if content doesn't change on a specific URL, the ETag will remain the same and the browser will use the cache. Figure 1-7 and Figure 1-8 include an example of the ETag response header. The code for this example is available in ch1/app.js.

If someone doesn't know what ETag is or how to use it, then it's better to leave the Express.js default etag setting as it is, which is on (boolean true). Otherwise, to disable ETag, use app.disable('etag');, which will eliminate the ETag HTTP response header.

---

[3]http://en.wikipedia.org/wiki/HTTP_ETag

By default, Express.js uses "weak" ETag. Other possible values are `false` (no ETag), `true` (weak ETag), and `strong` (strong ETag). The last option (for advanced developers) that Express.js provides is using your own ETag algorithm:

```
app.set('etag', function (body, encoding) {
  return customEtag(body, encoding); // you define the customEtag function
})
```

If you're not familiar with what weak or strong means, here's the short explanation of the differences between these types of ETags: an identical strong ETag guarantees the response is byte-for-byte the same, while an identical weak ETag indicates that the response is semantically the same. So you'll get different levels of caching with weak and strong ETags. Of course, this is a very brief and vague explanation. Please do you own research if this topic is important for your project.

query parser

A *query string* is data sent in the URL after the question mark (for example, `?name=value&name2=value2`). This format needs to be parsed into JavaScript/Node.js object format before we can use it. Express.js automatically includes this query parsing for our convenience. It does so by enabling the `query parser` setting.

The default value for `query parser` is extended, which uses the qs module's functionality.[4] Other possible values are

- `false`: Disable parsing

- `true`: Uses qs

- `simple`: Uses the core querystring module's functionality (`http://nodejs.org/api/querystring.html`)

It's possible to pass your own function as an argument, in which case your custom function will be used for parsing instead of parsing libraries. If you pass your own function, your custom parsing function must take a string argument and return a JavaScript/Node.js object similar to the `parse` function's signature from the core querystring module.[5]

The following are examples in which we set `query parser` to use querystring, no parsing and a custom parsing function:

```
app.set('query parser', 'simple');
app.set('query parser', false);
app.set('query parser', customQueryParsingFunction);
```

---

[4]`https://github.com/hapijs/qs`
[5]`http://nodejs.org/api/querystring.html#querystring_querystring_parse_str_sep_eq_options`

subdomain offset

The subdomain offset setting controls the value returned by the req.subdomains property. This setting is useful when the app is deployed on multiple subdomains, such as http://ncbi.nlm.nih.gov.

By default, the last two "subdomains" (the two extreme right parts) in the hostname/URL are dropped and the rest are returned in reverse order in the req.subdomains; so for our example of http://ncbi.nlm.nih.gov, the resulting req.subdomains is ['nlm', 'ncbi'].

However, if the app has subdomain offset set to 3 by app.set('subdomain offset', 3);, the result of req.subdomains will be just ['ncbi'], because Express.js will drop the three (3) parts starting from the right (nlm, nih, and gov).

Environments

As many of you know, most applications don't run in a single environment. Those environments usually include at least development, testing and production. Each of the environments puts a different requirement on the app. For example, in development the app error messaging needs to be as verbose as possible, while in production it needs to be user friendly and not compromise any system or user's personally identifiable information (PII)[6] data to hackers

The code needs to accommodate different environments without us, the developers, having to modify it every time we deploy to a different environment.

Of course, we can write up some if else statements based on the process.env.NODE_ENV value; for example:

```
if ('development' === process.env.NODE_ENV) {
```

If the line above seems strange to you, keep in mind that it's the exact equivalent of process.env.NODE_ENV === 'development'. Alternatively, you can use process.env.NODE_ENV == 'development' which will convert the NODE_ENV to string for you, before the comparison (if for some reason it's not a string already).

```
  // Connect to development database
} else if ('production' === process.env.NODE_ENV) {
  // Connect to production database
}; // Continue for staging and preview environments
```

Or using the Express.js env param (refer to the "env" section earlier in the chapter):

```
// Assuming that app is a reference to Express.js instance
if ('development' === app.get('env')) {
  // Connect to development database
} else if ('production' === app.get('env')) {
  // Connect to production database
}; // Continue for staging and preview environments
```

---

[6]http://en.wikipedia.org/wiki/Personally_identifiable_information

Another example of app.get('env') is one from the skeleton Express.js Generator app. It applies a more verbose error handler (sends the whole stacktrace from the err object) for the development environment than one for production or any other environment:

```
if (app.get('env') === 'development') {
    app.use(function(err, req, res, next) {
        res.status(err.status || 500);
        res.render('error', {
            message: err.message,
            error: err
        });
    });
}
```

If the environment is anything but development, instead of the error handler above, Express.js will use this one in which no stacktraces are leaked to a user:

```
app.use(function(err, req, res, next) {
    res.status(err.status || 500);
    res.render('error', {
        message: err.message,
        error: {}
    });
});
```

APP.CONFIGURE

The app.configure() method, which allows for more elegant environmental configuration, is *deprecated* in Express.js 4.x. However, you should still know how it works, because you might encounter it in older projects.

When the app.configure() method is invoked with one parameter it applies the callback to **all** environments. For example, if you want to set an author email and app name for any environment, then you can write:

```
app.configure(function(){
    app.set('appName', 'Pro Express.js Demo App');
    app.set('authorEmail', 'hi@azat.co');
});
```

However, if we pass two parameters (or more) with the first being an environment and the last one is still a function, the code will be called only when the app is in those environment modes (e.g., development, production).

For example, you can set different dbUri values (database connection strings) for development and stage with these callbacks:

```
app.configure('development', function() {
  app.set('dbUri', 'mongodb://localhost:27017/db');
});
app.configure('stage', 'production', function() {
  app.set('dbUri', process.env.MONGOHQ_URL);
});
```

■ **Tip**   Express.js often uses the difference in the number of input parameters and their types to direct functions' behavior. Therefore, pay close attention to how you invoke your methods.

Now that you're familiar with the settings, here's the demo kitchen-sink application. In it we gathered all the aforementioned settings to illustrate the examples. As you inspect the code, notice the order of the configuration statements in the file! They must be after the var app instantiation, but before middleware and routes. Here's the full source code of the example server ch1/app.js:

```
var book = {name: 'Practical Node.js',
  publisher: 'Apress',
  keywords: 'node.js express.js mongodb websocket oauth',
  discount: 'PNJS15'
}
var express = require('express'),
  path = require('path');

var app = express();

console.log(app.get('env'));

app.set('view cache', true);
app.set('views', path.join(__dirname, 'views'));
app.set('view engine', 'jade');
app.set('port', process.env.PORT || 3000);

app.set('trust proxy', true);
app.set('jsonp callback name', 'cb');
app.set('json replacer', function(key, value){
```

```
  if (key === 'discount')
    return undefined;
  else
    return value;
});
app.set('json spaces', 4);

app.set('case sensitive routing', true);
app.set('strict routing', true);
app.set('x-powered-by', false);
app.set('subdomain offset', 3);
// app.disable('etag')

app.get('/jsonp', function(request, response){
  response.jsonp(book);
})
app.get('/json', function(request, response){
  response.send(book);
})
app.get('/users', function(request, response){
  response.send('users');
})
app.get('/users/', function(request, response){
  response.send('users/');
})
app.get('*', function(request, response){
  response.send('Pro Express.js Configurations');
})

if (app.get('env') === 'development') {
    app.use(function(err, req, res, next) {
        res.status(err.status || 500);
        res.render('error', {
            message: err.message,
            error: err
        });
    });
}
var server = app.listen(app.get('port'), function() {
  console.log('Express server listening on port ' + server.address().port);
});
```

Summary

In this chapter, we covered how to configure Express.js system settings using methods such as app.set(), app.disable(), and app.enable(). You learned how to get the settings values with app.get() and app.enabled() and app.disabled(). Then, we covered all the important Express.js settings, their meaning and values. You also saw that settings can be arbitrary and used for storing app-specific custom info (e.g., port number or app name).

In a structure of a typical Express.js app, the middleware goes after the configuration section in the main Express.js app file. Both third-party middleware and custom middleware are available to use with Express.js. When you write your own middleware, it's a way to reuse and organize the code.

There is abundance of third-party Express.js middleware modules on NPM. They can do many tasks from parsing to authentication. By using third-party middleware, you are enhancing and customizing the behavior of your application. So middleware can be considered as configuration of its own kind (configuration on steroids!). Read on to master the most commonly used middleware!

CHAPTER 2

■ ■ ■

Working with Middleware

Middleware is an amazingly useful pattern that allows developers to reuse code within their applications and even share it with others in the form of NPM modules. The essential definition of *middleware* is a function with three arguments: request (or req), response (res), and next. If you're writing your own middleware, you can use arbitrary names for arguments, but it's better to stick to the common naming convention. Here's an example of how to define your own middleware:

```
var myMiddleware = function (req, res, next) {
  // Do something with req and/or res
  next();
};
```

When writing your own middleware, don't forget to call the next() callback function. Otherwise, the request will hang and time out. The request (req) and response (res) objects are the same for the subsequent middleware, so you can add properties to them (e.g., req.user = 'Azat') to access them later.

In this chapter we'll cover the following topics:

- *Applying middleware*: How to use middleware in Express.js apps

- *Essential middleware*: The most commonly used middleware, Connect.js middleware, and the middleware that was part of Express.js before version 4.x

- *Other middleware*: The most useful and popular third-party middleware

Unlike a traditional technical book chapter that describes how to build a single large project, this chapter extensively describes the most popular and used middleware modules. Similar to Chapter 1, this chapter is something akin to a reference. To demo you the middleware's features, there's a kitchen sink—meaning it has lots of different things—example in the ch2 folder. As usual, the code will be listed in the book and available in the GitHub repo at https://github.com/azat-co/express-api-ref.

Applying Middleware

To set up middleware, we use the app.use() method from the Express.js API. This is applicable to both third-party middleware and in-house middleware.

The method app.use() has one optional string parameter path and one mandatory function parameter callback. For example, to implement a logger with a date, time, request method, and URL, we use the console.log() method:

```
// Instantiate the Express.js app
app.use(function(req, res, next) {
  console.log('%s %s - %s', (new Date).toString(), req.method, req.url);
  return next();
});
// Implement server routes
```

On the other hand, if we want to prefix the middleware, a.k.a. *mounting*, we can use the path parameter, which restricts the use of this particular middleware to only the routes that have such a prefix. For example, to limit the logging to only the admin dashboard route /admin, we can write

```
// Instantiate the Express.js app
app.use('/admin', function(req, res, next) {
  console.log('%s %s - %s', (new Date).toString(), req.method, req.url);
  return next();
});
// Actually implement the /admin route
```

Writing everything from scratch, even as trivial as logging and serving of the static files, is obviously not much fun. Therefore, instead of implementing our own modules, we can utilize express.static() and morgan middleware functions. Here's an example of using express.static() and morgan middleware:

```
var express = require('express');
var logger = require('morgan');
// Instantiate and configure the app
app.use(logger('combined'));
app.use(express.static(__dirname + '/public'));
// Implement server routes
```

■ **Note** In Express.js version 3.x and earlier (i.e., before version 4.x), logger was part of Express.js and could be called with express.logger().

Static is the only middleware that remains bundled with Express.js version 4.x. Its NPM module is serve-static. Static middleware enables pass-through requests for static assets. Those assets are typically stored in the public folder (please refer to the Chapter 2 of Pro Express.js (Apress, 2014) for more information on recommended folder structure).

Here's a more advanced static middleware example that restricts assets to their respective folders. This is called mounting and achieved by providing two arguments to app.use(): route path and middleware function:

```
app.use('/css', express.static(__dirname + '/public/css'));
app.use('/img', express.static(__dirname + '/public/images'));
app.use('/js', express.static(__dirname + '/public/javascripts'));
```

A global path avoids ambiguity, which is why we use __dirname.

The pattern that static middleware is using behind the scenes is another good trick to have in your sleeves when you write your own middleware. This is now how it works: if you look closely, express.static() accepts a folder name as a parameter. This enables the middleware to change its behavior or modes dynamically. This pattern is called a monad, although people familiar with functional programming might argue that monad is something different. Anyway, the main idea here is that we have a function that stores data and returns another function.

The way this pattern is implemented in JavaScript/Node.js and modules like serve-static is with the return keyword. Here's an example where a custom myMiddleware function takes a parameter, and returns either different middleware A or the default middleware depending on whether or not the argument deep equals (===) to A:

```
var myMiddleware = function (param) {
  if (param === 'A') {
    return function(req, res, next) { // <---Middleware A
      // Do A stuff
      return next();
    }
  } else {
    return function(req, res, next) { // The default middleware
      // Do default stuff
      return next();
    }
  }
}
```

The ch2/app.js example, shown next, demonstrates how to apply (app.use()) the middleware static, morgan and other. The parameters and routes for each middleware used in the example are covered in their respective sections.

The full source code of the ch2/app.js to demo how to apply middleware (and to give you something working for the other middleware modules):

```
// Import and instantiate dependencies
var express = require('express'),
  path = require('path'),
  fs = require('fs'),
  compression = require('compression'),
  logger = require('morgan'),
  timeout = require('connect-timeout'),
  methodOverride = require('method-override'),
  responseTime = require('response-time'),
  favicon = require('serve-favicon'),
  serveIndex = require('serve-index'),
  vhost = require('vhost'),
  busboy = require('connect-busboy'),
  errorhandler = require('errorhandler');

var app = express();
// Configure settings
app.set('view cache', true);
app.set('views', path.join(__dirname, 'views'));
app.set('view engine', 'jade');
app.set('port', process.env.PORT || 3000);
app.use(compression({threshold: 1}));
app.use(logger('combined'));
app.use(methodOverride('_method'));
app.use(responseTime(4));
app.use(favicon(path.join('public', 'favicon.ico')));
// Apply middleware
app.use('/shared', serveIndex(
  path.join('public','shared'),
  {'icons': true}
));
app.use(express.static('public'));
// Define routes
app.use('/upload', busboy({immediate: true }));
app.use('/upload', function(request, response) {
  request.busboy.on('file', function(fieldname, file, filename, encoding,
  mimetype) {
    file.on('data', function(data){
      fs.writeFile('upload' + fieldname + filename, data);
    });
    file.on('end', function(){
      console.log('File ' + filename + ' is ended');
    });

  });
```

```
  request.busboy.on('finish', function(){
    console.log('Busboy is finished');
    response.status(201).end();
  })
});

app.get(
  '/slow-request',
  timeout('1s'),
  function(request, response, next) {
    setTimeout(function(){
      if (request.timedout) return false;
      return next();
    }, 999 + Math.round(Math.random()));
  }, function(request, response, next) {
    response.send('ok');
  }
);

app.delete('/purchase-orders', function(request, response){
  console.log('The DELETE route has been triggered');
  response.status(204).end();
});

app.get('/response-time', function(request, response){
  setTimeout(function(){
    response.status(200).end();
  }, 513);
});

app.get('/', function(request, response){
  response.send('Pro Express.js Middleware');
});
app.get('/compression', function(request, response){
  response.render('index');
})
// Apply error handlers
app.use(errorhandler());
// Boot the server
var server = app.listen(app.get('port'), function() {
  console.log('Express server listening on port ' + server.address().port);
});
```

Now that you know how to apply both third-party and in-house middleware, the next step is to identify which third-party middleware is essential. And what is available to developers and allows them to save themselves and teammates from the *"fun"* of implementing, maintaining, and testing the functionality that the NPM modules provide.

25

Essential Middleware

As you've seen in the previous section, middleware is nothing more than a function that takes req and res objects. Express.js version 4.x provides only one middleware function out of the box: express.static(). Most of the middleware needs to be installed and imported. The essential middleware usually stems from Sencha's Connect library: http://www.senchalabs.org/connect/ (NPM: https://npmjs.org/package/connect; GitHub: https://github.com/senchalabs/connect).

The main thing to remember when using middleware is that the order in which middleware functions are applied with the app.use() function matters, *because this is the order in which they'll be executed.* In other words, developers need to be cautious about the sequence of the middleware statements (in app.js), because this sequence will dictate the order in which each request will go through the corresponding middleware functions.

Are you confused already? Look at this example: a session (express-session) must follow a cookie (cookie-parser), because any web session depends on the cookies for storing the session ID (and it is provided by cookie-parser). If we move them around the sessions won't work! Another example is Cross-Site Request Forgery middleware csurf that requires express-session.

To make the point completely clear, middleware statements go before routes for the exact same reason. If you put static (express.static() or serve-static) middleware after a route definition, then the framework will finish the request flow by responding and the static assets (e.g., from /public) won't be served to the client.

Let's dig deeper into the following middleware:

- compression
- morgan
- body-parser
- cookie-parser
- express-session
- csurf
- express.static or serve-static
- connect-timeout
- errorhandler
- method-override
- response-time
- serve-favicon
- serve-index
- vhost
- connect-busboy

compression

The compression middleware (NPM: http://npmjs.org/compression) gzips transferred data. Gzip or GNU zip is a compression utility. To install compression v1.0.11, run this command in your terminal in the project's root folder:

```
$ npm install compression@1.0.11 --save
```

Do you remember that the order of the middleware statements matters? That's why the compression middleware is usually placed at the very beginning of an Express.js app configuration so that it precedes the other middleware and routes. The compression is utilized with the compression() method:

```
var compression = require('compression');
// ... Typical Express.js set up...
app.use(compression());
```

■ **Tip**   You need to install the compression NPM module in the project (i.e., local) node_modules folder. You can do so with $ npm install compression@1.0.10 --save or by putting the line "compression": "1.0.10" into the package.json file and running $ npm install.

The compression() method is good to go without any extra parameters, but if you are an advanced Node.js programmer, you may want to use the gzip options for compression:

- threshold: The size in kilobits at which to start compression (i.e., the minimum size in kilobits that can go uncompressed)
- filter: Function to filter out what to compress; the default filter is compressible, available at https://github.com/expressjs/compressible.

Gzip uses the core Node.js module zlib (http://nodejs.org/api/zlib.html#zlib_options) and just passes these options to it:

- chunkSize: Size of the chunks to use (default: 16*1024)
- windowBits: Window size
- level: Compression level
- memLevel: How much memory to allocate
- strategy: What gzip compression algorithm to apply
- filter: Function that by default tests for the Content-Type header to be json, text, or javascript

For more information on these options, please see the zlib docs at
http://zlib.net/manual.html#Advanced.

In the ch2 project, we create an index.jade file with some dummy text, then add the
following to the app.js file:

```
var compression = require('compression');
// ... Configurations
app.use(compression({threshold: 1}));
```

The views/index.jade file will render h1 and p HTML elements with some Lorem
Ipsum text, as follows:

```
h1 hi
p Lorem Ipsum is simply dummy text of ...
```

■ **Tip**   For a thorough Jade template engine tutorial, consult *Practical Node.js* (Apress, 2014).

As a result of applying compression, in the Chrome browser Developer Tools console
you can see the Content-Encoding: gzip response header, as shown in Figure 2-1.

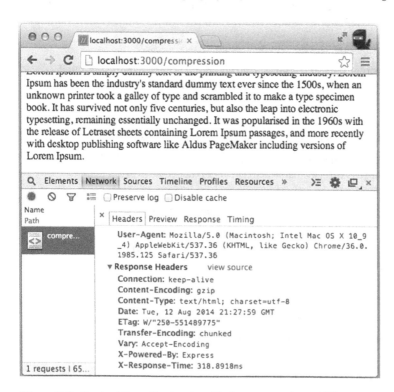

Figure 2-1.   *Content-Encoding is gzip with the compression middleware in use*

morgan

The morgan middleware (https://www.npmjs.org/package/morgan) keeps track of all the requests and other important information depending on the output format specified. To install morgan v1.2.2, use

```
$ npm install morgan@1.2.2 --save
```

Morgan takes either an options object or a format string (common, dev, etc.); for example,

```
var logger = require('morgan');
// ... Configurations
app.use(logger('common'));
```

or

```
var logger = require('morgan');
// ... Configurations
app.use(logger('dev'));
```

or

```
var logger = require('morgan');
// ... Configurations
app.use(logger(':method :url :status :res[content-length] - :response-time ms'));
```

Supported options to pass to the morgan function (logger() in the previous example) are as follows:

- format: A string with an output format; see the upcoming list of token string and predefined formats.

- stream: The output stream to use defaults to stdout, but could be anything else, such as a file or another stream.

- buffer: The number of milliseconds for the buffer interval; defaults to 1000ms if not set or not a number.

- immediate: Boolean value, that when set to true, makes the logger (morgan) write log lines on request instead of response.

The following are the available format string parameters or tokens:

- :req[header] (e.g., :req[Accept])

- :res[header] (e.g., :res[Content-Length])

- :http-version

- :response-time

- :remote-addr
- :date
- :method
- :url
- :referrer
- :user-agent
- :status

The following are the predefined formats/tokens that come with Morgan:

- combined: Same as :remote-addr - :remote-user [:date] ":method :url HTTP/:http-version" :status :res[content-length] ":referrer" ":user-agent"

- common: Same as :remote-addr - :remote-user [:date] ":method :url HTTP/:http-version" :status :res[content-length]

- short: Same as :remote-addr :remote-user :method :url HTTP/:http-version :status :res[content-length] - :response-time ms

- tiny: Same as :method :url :status :res[content-length] - :response-time ms

- dev: Short and colored development output with response statuses, same as :method :url :status :response-time ms - :res[content-length]

You could also define your own formats. For more information, please refer to the morgan documentation at https://www.npmjs.org/package/morgan.

body-parser

The body-parser module (https://www.npmjs.org/package/body-parser) is probably the most essential of all the third-party middleware modules. It allows developers to process incoming data, such as body payload, into usable JavaScript/Node.js objects. To install body-parser v1.6.1, run this command:

```
$ npm install body-parser@1.6.1
```

The body-parser module has the following distinct middleware:

- json(): Processes JSON data; e.g., {"name": "value", "name2": "value"}

- urlencoded(): Processes URL-encoded data; e.g., name=value&name2=value2

- raw(): Returns body as a buffer type

- text(): Returns body as string type

If the request has a MIME type of application/json, the json() middleware will try to parse the request payload as JSON. The result will be put in the req.body object and passed to the next middleware and routes.

We can pass the following options as properties:

- strict: Boolean true or false; if it's true (default), then a 400 status error (Bad Request) will be passed to the next() callback when the first character is not [or {.

- reviver: A second parameter to the JSON.parse() function that transforms the output; more info is available at MDN.[1]

- limit: Maximum byte size; disabled by default.

- inflate: Inflates the deflated body; default is true.

- type: Content-Type to parse; default is json.

- verify: A function to verify the body.

For example, if you need to skip the private methods/properties (by convention they begin with the underscore symbol, _), apply nonstrict parsing, and have a limit of 5,000 bytes, you could enter the following:

```
var bodyParser = require('body-parser');
// ... Express.js app set up
app.use(bodyParer.json({
  strict: false,
  reviver: function(key, value) {
    if (key.substr(0,1) === '_') {
      return undefined;
    } else {
      return value;
    }
  },
  limit: 5000
}));
// ...Boot-up
```

---

[1]https://developer.mozilla.org/en-US/docs/Web/JavaScript/Reference/Global_Objects/JSON/parse

urlencoded()

This body-parser module's urlencoded() middleware parses *only* requests with the x-ww-form-urlencoded header. It utilizes the qs module's (https://npmjs.org/package/qs) querystring.parse() function and puts the resulting JS object into req.body.

In addition to limit, type, verify, and inflate, urlencoded() takes an extended boolean option. The extended option is a *mandatory* field. When it is set to true (the default value), body-parser uses the qs module (https://www.npmjs.org/package/qs) to parse query strings.

If you set extended to false, body-parser uses the core Node.js module querystring for parsing of URL-encoded data. I recommend setting extended to true (that is, to use qs) because it allows objects and arrays to be parsed from URL-encoded strings.

If you forget what a URL-encoded string looks like, it's a name=value&name2=value2 string after the question mark (?) in the URL.

We can also pass the limit parameter to urlencoded(). The limit option works similarly to the limit in the bodyParser.json() middleware which you saw in the previous code snippet. For example, to set the limit to 10,000:

```
var bodyParser = require('body-parser');
// ... Express.js set up
app.use(bodyParser.urlencoded({limit: 10000}));
```

■ **Caution**   In older versions, bodyParser.multipart() middleware is known to be prone to malfunctioning when handling large file uploads. The exact problem is described by Andrew Kelley in the article "Do Not Use bodyParser with Express.js."[2] The current versions of Express.js v 4.x unbundled support for bodyParser.multipart(). Instead, the Express.js team recommends using busboy,[3] formidable,[4] or multiparty.[5]

---

cookie-parser

The cookie-parser middleware (https://www.npmjs.org/package/cookie-parser) allows us to access user cookie values from the req.cookie object in request handlers. The method takes a string, which is used for signing cookies. Usually, it's some clever pseudo-random sequence (e.g., very secret string). To install cookie-parser v1.3.2, run this command:

```
$ npm install cookie-parser@1.3.2
```

---

[2]http://andrewkelley.me/post/do-not-use-bodyparser-with-express-js.html
[3]https://www.npmjs.org/package/busboy
[4]https://www.npmjs.org/package/formidable
[5]https://www.npmjs.org/package/multiparty

Use it like this:

```
var cookieParser = require('cookie-parser');
// ... Some Express.js set up
app.use(cookieParser());
```

or with the secret string (arbitrary random string, usually stored in an environment variable):

```
app.use(cookieParser('cats and dogs can learn JavaScript'));
```

■ **Caution** *Avoid* storing any sensitive information in cookies, especially user-related information (personally identifiable information) such as credentials or their preferences. In most cases, use cookies only to store a unique and hard-to-guess key (session ID) that matches a value on the server. That enables you to retrieve a user session on subsequent requests.

In addition to secret, the cookieParser() also takes these options as a second parameter:

- path: A cookie path
- expires: Absolute expiration date for the cookie
- maxAge: Relative maximum age of the cookie
- domain: The web site domain for the cookie
- secure: Boolean indicating whether the cookie is secure or not
- httpOnly: Boolean indicating whether HTTP only or not

cookie-parser has some additional methods:

- JSONCookie(string): Parse string into a JSON data format
- JSONCookies(cookies): Same as JSONCookie(string) but for objects
- signedCookie(string, secret): Parse a cookie value as a signed cookie
- signedCookies(cookies, secret): Same as signedCookie(string, secret) but for objects

express-session

The express-session middleware (https://www.npmjs.org/package/express-session) allows the server to use web sessions. This middleware *must have* cookie-parser enabled before its definition (higher in the app.js file). To install express-session v1.7.6, run this command:

```
$ npm install express-session@1.7.6 --save
```

The express-session v1.7.6 middleware takes these options:

- key: Cookie name, defaulting to connect.sid

- store: Session store instance, usually a Redis object (covered in detail in Chapter 12 of Pro Express.js (Apress, 2014))

- secret: Used to sign the session cookie, to prevent tampering; usually just a random string

- cookie: Session cookie settings, defaulting to { path: '/', httpOnly: true, maxAge: null }

- proxy: Boolean that indicates whether to trust the reverse proxy when setting secure cookies (via "X-Forwarded-Proto")

- saveUninitialized: Boolean that forces the saving of a new session (default is true)

- unset: Controls if you want to keep the session in the store after unsetting the session with possible values keep and destroy (default is keep)

- resave: Boolean that forces the saving of the unmodified session (default is true)

- rolling: Boolean that sets a new cookie on each request which resets the expiration (default is false)

- genid: A function that generates session ID (default is uid2: https://www.npmjs.org/package/uid2, https://github.com/coreh/uid2)

By default, sessions are stored in the memory. However, we can use Redis for persistence and for sharing sessions between multiple machines. For more information on Express.js sessions, please refer to Pro Express.js (Apress, 2014) Part 3, particularly Chapter 12.

csurf

Cross-site request forgery (CSRF) occurs when a client still has session information from a protected web site, such as a bank's web site, and a malicious script submits data on the client's behalf, which could even be a money transfer. The attack succeeds because the bank's server can't distinguish between the client's valid request from the bank's web site and the malicious request from some compromised or untrustworthy web site. The browser has the right session, but the user wasn't on the bank's website's page!!!

To prevent CSRF, we can enable CSRF protection by using a token with each request and validating that token against our records. This way we know that we served the page or resource from which the subsequent request with submitted data is coming. For more information, please refer to the Wikipedia CSRF entry at http://en.wikipedia.org/wiki/Cross-site_request_forgery.

The CSRF protection with the csurf module (https://www.npmjs.org/package/csurf) is handled by Express.js by putting a _csrf token in the session (req.session._csrf) and validating that value against values in req.body, req.query, and the X-CSRF-Token header. If the values don't match, the 403 Forbidden HTTP status code is returned, which means that the resource is forbidden (see, e.g., http://en.wikipedia.org/wiki/HTTP_403). The csurf middleware doesn't check GET, HEAD, or OPTIONS methods by default. To install csurf v1.6.0, run this command:

```
$ npm install csurf@1.6.0 --save
```

The most minimal examples of using csurf v1.6.0 is as follows:

```
var csrf = require('csurf');
// ... Instantiate Express.js application
app.use(csrf());
```

The csurf v1.6.0 takes the following additional parameters:

- value: A function that takes request (req) as an argument, checks for the presense of the token, and returns the value true (found) or false (not found). Look at the example below.

- cookie: Specifies to use the cookie-based store instead of the default session-based one (not recommended)

- ignoreMethods: An array of HTTP methods to ignore when checking for the CSRF token in requests (default value is ['GET', 'HEAD', 'OPTIONS'])

You can override the default function that checks the token value presence by passing a callback function in a value property; for example, to use a different name and check against *only* the request body, you can use

```
var csrf = require('csurf');
// ... Instantiate Express.js application
app.use(express.csrf({
  value: function (req) {
    return (req.body && req.body.cross_site_request_forgery_value);
  }
}));
```

The csrf middleware must be after express-session, cookie-parser, and optionally (meaning if you plan to support tokens in the body of requests) after body-parser middlewares:

```
var bodyParser = require('body-parser');
var cookieParser = require('cookie-parser');
var session = require('express-session');
var csrf = require('csurf');
// ... Instantiate Express.js application
app.use(bodyParser.json());
app.use(cookieParser());
app.use(session());
app.use(csrf());
```

express.static( )

The express.static() or serve-static as a stand-alone module (https://www.npmjs.org/package/serve-static) is the only middleware that comes with Express.js version 4.x, so you don't have to install it. In other words, under the hood, express.static() is a serve-static module: https://github.com/expressjs/serve-static. We already covered the express.static(path, options) method that serves files from a specified root path to the folder, such as:

```
app.use(express.static(path.join(__dirname, 'public')));
```

or (not recommended because this might not work on Windows):

```
app.use(express.static(__dirname + '/public'));
```

A relative path is also an option:

```
app.use(express.static('public'));
```

The express.static(path, options) v1.5.0 (for Express.js v4.8.1) method takes these options:

- maxAge: Number of milliseconds to set for browser cache maxAge, which defaults to 0

- redirect: Boolean true or false (default is true) indicating whether to allow a redirect to a trailing slash (/) when the URL pathname is a directory

- dotfiles: Indicates how to treat hidden system folders/files (e.g., .gitignore); possible values are ignore (default), allow, and deny

- etag: Boolean indicating whether or not to use ETag caching (default is true)

- extensions: Boolean indicating whether or not to use the default file extensions (default is false)

- index: Identifies the index file; default is index.html; an array, a string and false (disable) are possible values

- setHeaders: A function to set custom response headers

Here's an example of the express.static() advanced usage with some arbitrary values:

```
app.use(express.static(__dirname + '/public', {
  maxAge: 86400000,
  redirect: false,
  hidden: true,
  'index': ['index.html', 'index.htm']
}));
```

connect-timeout

The connect-timeout module (https://www.npmjs.org/package/connect-timeout) sets a timeout. Use of this middleware is recommended only on specific routes (e.g., '/slow-route') that you suspect might be slower than average ones. To use connect-timeout v1.2.2, install it with:

```
$ npm install connect-timeout@1.2.2 --save
```

In your server file, write these statements as shown in example ch2/app.js:

```
var timeout = require('connect-timeout');
// ... Instantiation and configuration
app.get(
  '/slow-request',
  timeout('1s'),
  function(request, response, next) {
```

```
    setTimeout(function(){
      if (request.timedout) return false;
      return next();
    }, 999 + Math.round(Math.random()));
  }, function(request, response, next) {
    response.send('ok');
  }
);
// ... Routes and boot-up
```

Run the server with $ node app. Then, from the separate terminal, send a few GET requests with CURL:

```
$ curl http://localhost:3000/slow-request -i
```

The response should time out about half of the time with a 503 Service Unavailable status code. The good response returns status code 200. Both are shown in Figure 2-2. It's possible to customize the message in the error handlers.

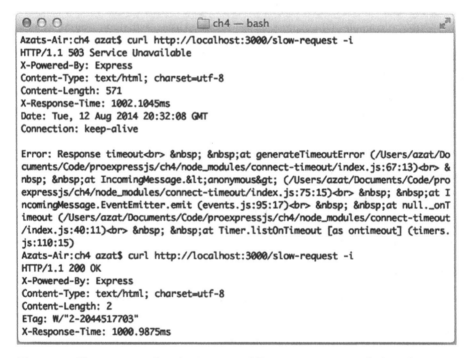

Figure 2-2. *The responses when the timeout middleware is in action and when it's not*

errorhandler

The errorhandler middleware (https://www.npmjs.org/package/errorhandler) can be used for basic error handling. This is especially useful in development and for prototyping. This module doesn't do anything that you can't do yourself with custom error-handling middleware. However, it will save you time. For production environments, please consider customizing error handling to your needs.

The errorhandler v1.1.1 module installation is done with the following NPM command:

```
$ npm install errorhandler@1.1.1 --save
```

We apply it in the server file like this:

```
var errorHandler = require('errorhandler');
// ... Configurations
app.use(errorHandler());
```

Or, only for development mode:

```
if (app.get('env') === 'development') {
  app.use(errorhandler());
}
```

It's trivial to write your own error handlers. For example, this is a primitive handler that renders an error template with an error message:

```
app.use(function(err, req, res, next) {
    res.status(err.status || 500);
    res.render('error', {
        message: err.message,
        error: {}
    });
});
```

As you can see, the method signature is similar to request handlers or middleware, but has four arguments instead of three, like middleware, or two, like a core Node.js request handler. This is how Express.js determines that this is an error handler and not middleware—four parameters in the function definition: error (err), request (req), response (res), and next.

This error handler is triggered from inside of the other middleware by calling next() with an error object; for example, next(new Error('something went wrong')). If we call next() without arguments, Express.js assumes that there were no errors and proceeds to the next middleware in the chain.

method-override

The method-override middleware (https://www.npmjs.org/package/method-override) enables your server to support HTTP methods that might be unsupported by clients—for example, systems where requests are limited to GET and POST (such as an HTML form in the browser). To install method-override v2.1.3, run:

```
$ npm install method-override@2.1.3 --save
```

The method-override module can use the X-HTTP-Method-Override=VERB header from the incoming requests:

```
var methodOverride = require('method-override');
// ... Configuratoins
app.use(methodOverride('X-HTTP-Method-Override'));
```

In addition to the header, we can use a query string. For example, to support requests with ?_method=VERB:

```
var methodOverride = require('method-override');
// ... Configuratoins
app.use(methodOverride('_method'));
```

In ch2/app.js, after we install, import, and apply the method-override middleware with the query string approach and _method name, we can define a DELETE route like this:

```
app.delete('/purchase-orders', function(request, response){
  console.log('The DELETE route has been triggered');
  response.status(204).end();
});
```

After we start the app with $ node app, we submit *the POST* request with CURL in a separate terminal window. In the URL, we specify the _method as DELETE:

```
$ curl http://localhost:3000/purchase-orders/?_method=DELETE -X POST
```

This CURL request is treated by Express.js as the DELETE HTTP method request, and we will see the following message on the server:

```
The DELETE route has been triggered
```

For Windows users, CURL can be installed from http://curl.haxx.se/download.html. Or, you can use jQuery's $.ajax() function from the Chrome Developer Tools.

response-time

The response-time middleware (https://www.npmjs.org/package/response-time)
adds the X-Response-Time header with the time in milliseconds from the moment the
request entered this middleware.

To install response-time v2.0.1, run

```
$ npm install response-time@2.0.1 --save
```

The response-time() method takes a number of digits after the point that need to be
included in the result (3 is the default). Let's ask for 4 digits:

```
var responseTime = require('response-time');
// ... Middleware
app.use(responseTime(4));
```

To illustrate this middleware in action, run ch2/app.js with $ node app. The server
has these statements pertaining to the response-time middleware:

```
app.use(responseTime(4));
// ... Middleware
app.get('/response-time', function(request, response){
  setTimeout(function(){
    response.status(200).end();
  }, 513);
});
```

The idea behind the preceding /response-time route is to delay the response by 513 ms.
Then, in a separate terminal window, run the curl command with -i to make a GET request
and output response information:

```
$ curl http://localhost:3000/response-time -i
```

As shown in Figure 2-3, this header appears in the response:

```
X-Response-Time: 514.3193ms
```

Figure 2-3. HTTP response with the X-Response-Time header that shows response time

serve-favicon

The serve-favicon middleware (https://www.npmjs.org/package/serve-favicon)
enables you to change the default favorite icon in the browser into a custom one.

To install the static-favicon v2.0.1 module, run:

```
$ npm install serve-favicon@2.0.1 --save
```

To include and apply the middleware, run

```
var favicon = require('serve-favicon');
// ... Instantiations
app.use(favicon(path.join(__dirname, 'public', 'favicon.ico')));
```

The serve-favicon v2.0.1 module has two parameters:

- path: The path to the favorite icon file, or Buffer with the icon data
  (Buffer is a Node.js binary type)

- options: maxAge in milliseconds—how long to cache the favorite
  icon; the default is 1 day

When you run ch2/app.js, you should see the webapplog.com logo on the tab, as
shown in Figure 2-4.

Figure 2-4. *Favorite icon with the serve-favicon middleware in use*

serve-index

The `serve-index` middleware (`https://www.npmjs.org/package/serve-index`) enables you to create a directory listing based on a particular folder's content. Think about it as a terminal $ `ls` command (or `dir` on Windows). You can even customize the look with your own template and style sheet (the options are discussed later in this section).

To install `serve-index` v1.1.6, run:

```
$ npm install serve-index@1.1.6 --save
```

To apply the middleware, write these lines in your server file:

```
var serveIndex = require('serve-index');
// ... Middleware
app.use('/shared', serveIndex(
  path.join('public','shared'),
  {'icons': true}
));
app.use(express.static('public'));
```

In the `serveIndex` statement, specify the `'/shared'` folder and pass the `path.join('public', 'shared')`; path to the `public/shared` folder in the project directory. A value of `true` for icons (`icons: true`) means to display icons. The static middleware is needed to display the actual file.

These lines of code are taken from `ch2/app.js`, and if you run it and navigate to `http://localhost:3000/shared`, you'll see a web interface with the folder name (`shared`) and file name (`abc.txt`) as shown in Figure 2-5.

Figure 2-5. *The default serve-index web interface with folder and a file*

If you resize the browser to be narrow enough, the interface should change—responsiveness! Also, there's the search bar thanks to the default serve-index interface.

Clicking the file name abc.txt should open the file displaying the message "secret text," as shown in Figure 2-6. This is a a result of using the expsess.static() middleware, and not serve-index.

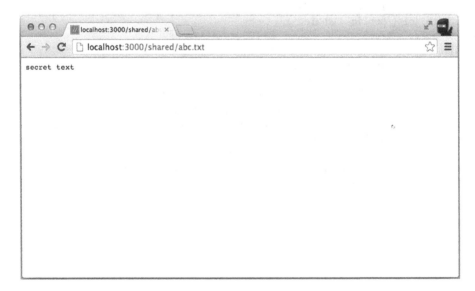

Figure 2-6. *Text file served by the static middleware*

The serve-index middleware takes an options object as a second parameter (the first is the path). The options can have the following properties:

- hidden: Boolean indicating whether or not to display hidden (dot) files; defaults to false

- view: Display mode (tiles or details); defaults to tiles

- icons: Boolean indicating whether or not to show icons next to file names/folder names; defaults to false

- filter: A filter function; defaults to false

- stylesheet: Path to a CSS style sheet (optional); defaults to the built-in style sheet

- template: Path to an HTML template (optional); defaults to the built-in template

In the template, you can use: {directory} for the name of the directory, {files} for the HTML of an unordered list (<ol>) of file links, {linked-path} for the HTML of a link to the directory, and {style} for the specified stylesheet and embedded images.

■ **Caution** Don't use serve-index liberally on system folders and secret files. It's good to keep it constrained to a certain subfolder, such as public.

---

vhost

The vhost middleware (https://www.npmjs.org/package/vhost) enables you to use a different routing logic based on the domain. For example, we can have two Express.js apps, api and web, to organize code for different routes based on the domain, api.hackhall.com or www.hackhall.com, respectively:

```
var app =express()
var api = express()
var web = express()
// ... Configurations, middleware and routes
app.use(vhost('www.hackhall.com', web))
app.use(vhost('api.hackhall.com', api))
app.listen(3000)
```

To install vhost v2.0.0, run:

```
$ npm install vhost@2.0.0 --save
```

The vhost v2.0.0 middleware takes two parameters (as shown in the previous example):

- domain: String or RegExp; for example, *.webapplog.com
- server: Server object (express or connect); for example, api or web

connect-busboy

The connect-busboy module (https://www.npmjs.org/package/connect-busboy) is connect.js/Express.js middleware that is built to be used with busboy form parser (https://www.npmjs.org/package/busboy). The busboy form parser basically takes the incoming HTTP(S) request multipart body and allows us to use its fields, uploaded files, and so forth. To install the connect-busboy v0.0.1 middleware, which already includes busboy, run

```
$ npm install connect-busboy@0.0.1 --save
```

Then, in your server file (app.js), write something similar to the following to implement a file upload functionality on the /upload route:

```
var busboy = require('connect-busboy');
// ... Configurations
app.use('/upload', busboy({immediate: true }));
app.use('/upload', function(request, response) {
  request.busboy.on('file', function(fieldname, file, filename, encoding,
  mimetype) {
    file.on('data', function(data){
      fs.writeFile('upload' + fieldname + filename, data);
    });
    file.on('end', function(){
      console.log('File ' + filename + ' is ended');
    });

  });
  request.busboy.on('finish', function(){
    console.log('Busboy is finished');
    response.status(201).end();
  })
});
```

The preceding example writes the file to the disk and outputs 201 to the client upon finishing. In the terminal, we should see the file name with the word "ended".

To simulate a file upload without the web page form, we can use our good old friend CURL (one-line command):

```
$ curl -X POST -i -F name=icon -F filedata=@./public/favicon.ico
  http://localhost:3000/upload
```

The file that we're uploading is in ch2/public/favicon.ico. This is the favorite icon from the earlier serve-favicon example. As a result, there should be a file named uploadfiledatafavicon.ico in the project folder. And in your terminal on the server window, you should see messages:

```
File favicon.ico is ended
Busboy is finished
```

In your terminal on the client (i.e., curl window), you'll see 201 Created.

■ **Note** In addition to the ch2 example, please see the chapters in Pro Express.js (Apress, 2014) Part 4 for more advanced examples on middleware.

Other Middleware

There are many other noteworthy modules that are compatible with Connect.js and Express.js. The following is only a brief list of some of the currently popular modules; many more are coming out every month, and some are being discontinued or abandoned, so check NPM for updates regularly. You can find each of these modules at https://www.npmjs.org/package/package *name*, where *package name* is the name of the module in the following list.

- cookies and kegrip: Alternatives to cookie-parser
  (https://www.npmjs.org/package/cookies,
  https://www.npmjs.org/package/keygrip,
  https://www.npmjs.org/package/cookie-parser)

- cookie-session: Cookie-based session store
  (https://www.npmjs.org/package/cookie-session)

- raw-body: For requests as buffers
  (https://www.npmjs.org/package/raw-body)

- connect-multiparty: Uses mutliparty and acts as an alternative to connect-busboy
  (https://www.npmjs.org/package/connect-multiparty,
  https://www.npmjs.org/package/multiparty,
  https://www.npmjs.org/package/connect-busboy)

- qs: Alternative to query and querystring
  (https://www.npmjs.org/package/qs,
  https://www.nodejs.org/api/querystring.html)

- st, connect-static, and static-cache: Caching of static assets
  (https://www.npmjs.org/package/st,
  https://www.npmjs.org/package/connect-static, and
  https://www.npmjs.org/package/static-cache)

- `express-validator`: Incoming data validation/sanitation (https://www.npmjs.org/package/express-validator)

- `everyauth` and `passport`: Authentication and authorization middleware (https://www.npmjs.org/package/everyauth and https://www.npmjs.org/package/passport)

- `oauth2-server`: OAuth2 server middleware (https://www.npmjs.org/package/oauth2-server)

- `helmet`: Collection of security middleware (https://www.npmjs.org/package/helmet)

- `connect-cors`: Cross-origin resource sharing (CORS) support for Express.js servers (https://www.npmjs.org/package/connect-cors)

- `connect-redis`: Redis session store for Express.js sessions (https://www.npmjs.org/package/connect-redis)

Summary

This chapter covered how to create and apply your own custom middleware and how to install and apply third-party middleware from NPM. You learned how the most essential middleware works, which parameters their functions take, and how they behave. You might have noticed that we used a small template for the error page and for the compression page in the `ch2` example project.

The next chapter is a continuation of the configuration and middleware theme. Those are distinct parts of virtually any Express.js app (or `server.js` or `index.js`, meaning the main Express.js file). The next topic is all about configuring views that are facilitated by templates. Chapter 3 is an immersion into how we can use different template engines. We explore how to utilize the most popular options with Express.js, such as Jade and Handlebars, and other libraries.

CHAPTER 3

■ ■ ■

Template Engines and Consolidate.js

Template engines are libraries that allow us to use different template languages (EJS, Handlebars, Jade, etc.). But what is a template language? Template language is a special set of instructions (syntax and control structures) that tells the engine how to process data. The language is specific to a particular template engine. The instructions in the template are usually used to present data in a better format suitable for end-users. In the case of web apps such final representation format is HTML. So basically, we have some data (JSON or JavaScript/Node.js objects), and templates (EJS, Handlebars, Jade, etc.). When they are combined, we get the output, which is good old HTML.

The process of combining data with templates is called *rendering*. Some template engines have functionality to *compile* templates as an extra step before rendering. Compilation is similar to caching and is geared towards optimizing for frequent reuse.

"Why the heck use templates?" you might ask if you haven't used them before. There are multiple advantages of using templates over not using them, the most important of which is that you can reuse code—for example, menus, headers, footers, buttons and other form elements, and so forth. This way, if you need to make a change later, you'll have to update code in only one place instead of changing it in every file. Another advantage is that, depending on what library you're using, you can make templates more dynamic. This means that you can add some logic to the template and make it smarter (e.g., a for loop to iterate over each row of the table).

Jade allows pretty much any JavaScript/Node.js in its code; that is, the developers can harness the full power of rich JavaScript API in the templates!

This comes as a startling contrast to the approach used by Handlebars, which won't allow you to use JavaScript/Node.js functions in its templates. Although Handlebars' philosophy is to limit standard functions, it allows registering custom functions in the JavaScript/Node.js code (i.e., outside of the template itself).

Embedded JavaScript (EJS) is another popular choice for Node.js apps and it might be a better alternative when performance is important because in benchmark tests EJS performs better than Jade. Most of these template engines are suited for both browser JavaScript and Node.js.

In this chapter we'll cover the following topics:

- How to use template engines: Plugging different template engines into Express.js projects
- Uncommon libraries: Using rare template engines with Express.js
- Template engine choices: Different stand-alone template engine libraries
- Consolidate.js: a one-stop library for seamless integration of virtually all template engines with Express.js

How to Use Template Engines

Some of the examples from the previous chapters used these two configuration statements:

```
app.set('views', path);
app.set('view engine', name);
```

Or, with values:

```
var path = require('path')
// ... Configurations
app.set('views', path.join(__dirname, 'templates'));
app.set('view engine', 'ejs');
```

where path is a path to the folder with the templates, and name is a template filename extension and an NPM library name (e.g., jade is both an extension and an NMP name).

These two lines were enough to make Express.js render EJS or Jade templates. We didn't even have to import Jade in the app.js files. (But we still need to install the modules locally!) This is because, under the hood, the Express.js library imports the libraries based on the extension (the exact way it works is described in the next section of this chapter):

```
require('jade');
```

or

```
require('ejs');
```

There are two approaches to specifying a template engine extension:

- With the render() function
- With the view engine setting

Usually the file extension is the NPM module name for that template engine. Here's an example of the first approach where the extension can be simply put after the file name in the render function's argument:

```
response.render('index.jade');
```

The response.render is called inside of the route request handler. More details on render and other response object methods are provided later in the chapter.

If we use this approach (i.e., full file names with the extension), we can omit this line:

```
app.set('view engine', 'jade');
```

You can mix and match different template engines in one Express.js application.

Of course, the libraries that Express.js calls need to be installed in the local node_modules folder. For example, to install jade v1.5.0, we have to define it in the package.json and then run:

```
$ npm install
```

Here's the line from ch2/package.json:

```
"jade": "1.5.0",
```

To use any other template engine, make sure that you install that module with NPM, preferably by adding it to package.json as well, either manually or with npm install *name* --save.

Interestingly enough, Express.js uses views as the default value. Therefore, if you have templates in the views folder, you can omit this line:

```
app.set('views', path.join(__dirname, 'views'));
```

You know how to use app.set() for EJS and Jade templates, so now let's cover how to use alternative template engines with the configuration method: app.engine().

app.engine()

The app.engine() method is a lower-level method for setting up template engines. Express.js uses this method under the hood.

By default, Express.js will try to require a template engine based on the extension provided (the template engine NPM module name—that's why we use this name as the extension!). For example, when we call res.render('index.jade'); (more on this method later) in the request handler of the route or in middleware with the index.jade file name as an argument, the framework is calling require('jade') internally.

The full statement in the Express.js code (you don't need to implement it yourself just yet) is something like this: app.engine('jade', require('jade').__express);, where __express is a convention that template libraries should implement.

Let's say you prefer *.html or *.template instead of *.jade for your Jade files. In this case you can use app.set() and app.engine() to overwrite the default extension. For example, to use *.html, write these statements:

```
app.set('view engine', 'html');
app.engine('html', require('jade').__express);
```

and then, in each route, write something like this to render index.html:

```
response.render('index');
```

Or, for the '*.template' example, you can use an alternative approach without the view engine and with the full file name in the request handler (basically copying the internal Express.js code):

```
app.engine('template', require('jade').__express);
```

The following is the request handler call:

```
response.render('index.template');
```

This overwriting is especially cool for Handlebars and other template engines that take plain HTML, because you can reuse your legacy HTML files without much of a hassle.

Uncommon Libraries

Now let's cover the use of uncommon template engines. You can safely skip the rest of this section if you plan to use only common libraries such as Jade or EJS.

Less common Node.js choices of libraries need to expose the _express method, which is the common convention to indicate that a template library supports this Express.js format. So check if the template engine has __express() on the source file that you import with require(). If the __express() method is present, then the contributors made this library compatible with Express.js. Again, most of the libraries are already outfitted to work with Express.js and they have __express().

What if the library of your choice doesn't have __express? If the template module has a method with a signature similar to the __express method signature, you can easily define your template engine's method with app.engine; for example, in swig (https://github.com/paularmstrong/swig), it's the renderFile() method. So, considering that renderFile in a template engine library of your choice supports a function signature with these arguments:

- path: Path to a template file

- locals: Data to use for rendering HTML

- callback: The callback function

you can write code like this to apply this library as Express.js middleware:

```
// ... Declare dependencies
// ... Instantiate the app
// ... Configure the app
app.engine('swig', require('swig').renderFile);
// ... Define the routes
```

The example in the ch3 folder shows how you can use multiple template engines and various extensions. This is the scoop of the app.js statements:

```
// ... Declare dependencies
// ... Instantiate the app
// ... Configure the app
var jade = require('jade');
var consolidate = require('consolidate');

app.engine('html', jade.__express);
app.engine('template', jade.__express);
app.engine('swig', consolidate.swig);
// ... Define the routes
app.get('/', function(request, response){
  response.render('index.html');
});

app.get('/template', function(request, response){
  response.render('index.template');
});

app.get('/swig', function(request, response){
  response.render('index.swig');
})
```

The consolidate library will be explained later in this chapter.

The package.json file has the following dependencies (install them with npm install):

```
{
  "name": "template-app",
  "version": "0.0.1",
  "private": true,
  "scripts": {
    "start": "node app"
  },
  "dependencies": {
    "consolidate": "^0.10.0",
    "errorhandler": "1.1.1",
```

```
      "express": "4.8.1",
      "jade": "1.5.0",
      "morgan": "1.2.2",
      "swig": "^1.4.2",
      "serve-favicon": "2.0.1"
  }
}
```

Starting the application with $ node app should start the server that will render "Hi, I'm Jade from index.html" when you go to the home page (see Figure 3-1).

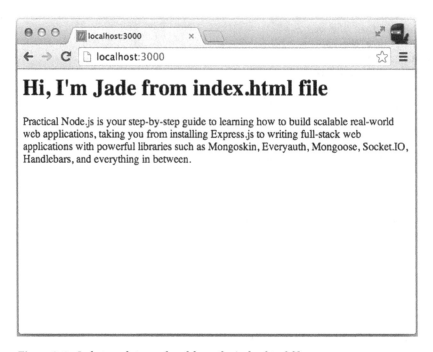

Figure 3-1. *Jade template rendered from the index.html file*

Also, the server should render "Hi, I'm Swig from index.swig" when you go to the /swig (see Figure 3-2).

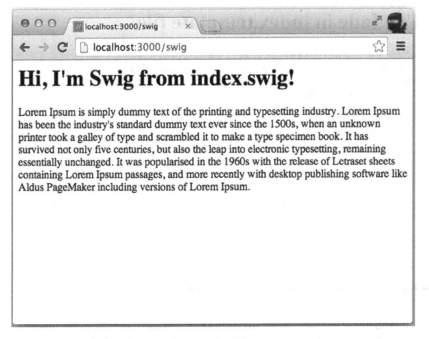

Figure 3-2. *Swig template rendered from the index.swig file*

And lastly, it should render "hi, I'm Jade in index.template file" when you go to the /template (see Figure 3-3).

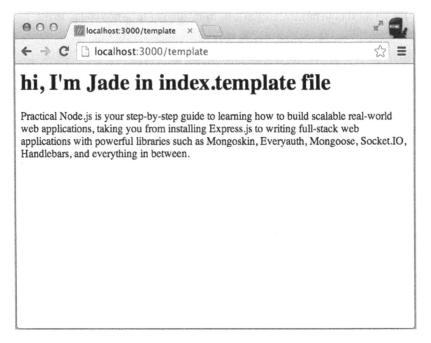

Figure 3-3. Jade template rendered from the index.jade file

This is probably an over-the-top example, because you will rarely use more than one template engine in a single Express.js app. However, it's good to know that the framework is flexible enough to allow you to implement it with just a few configuration statements.

It's worth noting, in our expressapiref/ch3 example, both Jade files index.html and index.template use the so-called top-down inclusion via include filename (without quotes). This allows us to reuse the Lorem Ipsum text of the paragraph in the lorem-ipsum.html file.

The file in our example is just a plain text file, but it can have Jade template content in it. The index.html looks like this:

```
h1 Hi, I'm Jade from index.html file
p
   include lorem-ipsum.html
```

And the index.temlate is similar:
```
h1 hi, I'm Jade in index.template file
p
   include lorem-ipsum.html
```

INCLUSIONS, LAYOUTS AND PARTIALS

Top-down inclusion is a standard inheritance pattern in which the parent object commands where and what to do with the child (the object that is included). So, for example, you have a file A that includes file B (a partial), and file A will do with file B what it wants. This is what you'll use in most template languages.

The alternative to top-down inclusion is the bottom-up pattern. Not all languages support it. In this case, file A is a larger and higher-up-the-chain entity (a layout), and file B is a smaller piece of the puzzle, but file B will dictate what it wants.

You can also think about the top-down approach as overwriting some methods in a child class when you extend those methods from the parent class, while leaving the others intact.

In Jade, bottom-up is implemented with a set of extend, layout, and block statements. For deep coverage on Jade, refer to *Practical Node.js* (Apress, 2014).

Template Engine Choices

This section briefly introduces the libraries that support Express.js without any modifications. This list of choices is derived from the list at the Express.js wiki page: https://github.com/strongloop/express/wiki#template-engines.

Jade

Jade (https://github.com/jadejs/jade) is a Haml-inspired template engine. It's very powerful because it has two types of inheritances, supports all JavaScript/Node.js, and requires a minimum number of symbols/characters due to treating whitespace and indentation as part of the language.

Haml.js

Haml.js (https://github.com/tj/haml.js) is a Haml implementation. Haml is a standard choice for Rails developers. This language treats whitespace and indentation as part of the language, which makes code more compact and less prone to typos, thus making it more pleasurable to write.

EJS

EJS (https://github.com/tj/ejs) is an embedded JavaScript template engine. According to some benchmark performance tests, EJS is faster than Jade or Haml (see, for example, http://paularmstrong.github.io/node-templates/benchmarks.html).

Handlebars.js

Hbs (https://github.com/donpark/hbs) is an adapter for Handlebars.js, which is an extension of the Mustache.js template engine. By design, Handlebars prohibits putting complex logic in the templates. Instead, developers need to write functions outside of templates and register them. This is the easiest template engine to learn. It's often used in reactive templates. If you're familiar with (or plan to use) Angular.js, Meteor, or DerbyJS, this choice might be better for you because it is similar to what they use.

Alternative adapter is express-hbs (https://github.com/barc/express-hbs) which is the Handlebars with layouts, partials. blocks for Express 3 from Barc (http://barc.com).

Another adapter is express-handlebars (https://github.com/ericf/express-handlebars).

Hogan.js Adapters

h4e (https://github.com/tldrio/h4e) is an adapter for Hogan.js, with support for partials and layouts. Hulk-hogan (https://github.com/quangv/hulk-hogan) is an adapter for Twitter's Hogan.js (Mustache syntax), with support for partials.

Combyne.js

The Combyne.js (https://github.com/tbranyen/combyne.js) is a template engine that hopefully works the way you'd expect. And combynexpress (https://github.com/tbranyen/combynexpress) is an Express library for Combyne.js.

Swig

Swig (https://github.com/paularmstrong/swig) is a fast, Django-like template engine.

Whiskers

Whiskers (https://github.com/gsf/whiskers.js) is small, fast, and mustachioed (looks like Handlebars or Mustache). It is faster than Jade (per http://paularmstrong.github.io/node-templates/benchmarks.html).

Blade

Blade (https://github.com/bminer/node-blade) is an HTML template compiler, inspired by Jade and Haml that treats whitespace as part of the language.

Haml-Coffee

Haml-Coffee (`https://github.com/netzpirat/haml-coffee`) provides Haml templates in which you can write inline CoffeeScript. It is perfect if you're using CoffeeScript for your Node.js code (the benefits of CoffeeScript are highlighted in this presentation: `http://www.infoq.com/presentations/coffeescript-lessons`).

Webfiller

Webfiller (`https://github.com/haraldrudell/webfiller`) is a plain HTML5 dual-side rendering engine with self-configuring routes, organized source tree. Webfiller is 100% JS.

Consolidate.js

In case the template engine of your choice does not provide an __express() method, or you're not sure and don't want to bother finding out, consider the consolidate library (`https://npmjs.org/package/consolidate`; GitHub: `https://github.com/tj/consolidate.js`).

The consolidate library streamlines and generalizes a few dozen template engine modules so that they "play nicely" with Express.js. This means there's no need to look up the source code to search for the presence of the __express() method. All you need to do is require consolidate and then map the engine of your choice to the extension.

Here is a Consolidate.js example:

```
var express = require('express');
var consolidate = require('consolidate');

var app = express();

// ... configure template engine:
app.engine('html', consolidate.handlebars);
app.set('view engine', 'html');
app.set('views', __dirname + '/views');
```

That's it; res.render() is ready to use Handlebars!

The template engines that Consolidate.js supports, as of this writing, are shown in Table 3-1 (compiled from the Consolidate.js GitHub page:

`https://github.com/tj/consolidate.js/blob/master/Readme.md`).

Table 3-1. *Template Engines Supported by Consolidate.js*

Template Engine	GitHub	Web Site (if applicable)
atpl	https://github.com/soywiz/atpl.js	
dust	https://github.com/akdubya/dustjs	http://akdubya.github.io/dustjs/
eco	https://github.com/sstephenson/eco	
ect	https://github.com/baryshev/ect	http://ectjs.com
ejs	https://github.com/tj/ejs	http://www.embeddedjs.com
haml	https://github.com/tj/haml.js	http://haml.info
haml-coffee	https://github.com/9elements/haml-coffee	http://haml.info
handlebars.js	https://github.com/wycats/handlebars.js/	http://handlebarsjs.com
Hogan.js	https://github.com/twitter/hogan.js	http://twitter.github.io/hogan.js
Jade	https://github.com/jadejs/jade	http://jade-lang.com
jazz	https://github.com/shinetech/jazz	
jqtpl	https://github.com/kof/jqtpl	
JUST	https://github.com/baryshev/just	
liquor	https://github.com/chjj/liquor	
lodash	https://github.com/lodash/lodash	https://lodash.com
mustache	https://github.com/janl/mustache.js	http://mustache.github.io
nunjunks	http://mozilla.github.io/nunjucks/	
QEJS	https://github.com/jepso/QEJS	
ractive	https://github.com/ractivejs/ractive	

(*continued*)

Table 3-1. (*continued*)

Template Engine	GitHub	Web Site (if applicable)
swig	https://github.com/paularmstrong/swig	http://paularmstrong.github.com/swig/
templayed	http://archan937.github.io/templayed.js/	
toffee	https://github.com/malgorithms/toffee	
underscore	https://github.com/jashkenas/underscore	http://documentcloud.github.io/underscore/
walrus	https://github.com/jeremyruppel/walrus	http://documentup.com/jeremyruppel/walrus/
whiskers	https://github.com/gsf/whiskers.js/	

Jade template language is quite extensive in itself and is beyond the scope of this book. To learn about every feature and the differences between extend and include (top-down and bottom-up), refer to *Practical Node.js* (Apress, 2014), which has a whole chapter dedicated to Jade and Handlebars.

Summary

Templates are a staple of modern web development. Without them developers would have to write way more code and the maintenance would be painful. When it comes to Node.js, Jade—a close relative to Ruby on Rails' Haml—is a powerful choice. This is due to its rich set of features and elegance of style (whitespaces and indentations are part of the language). But don't attempt to write Jade without learning it first. It might be painful.

Express.js supports different approaches to configuring the location of templates and file extensions. Also, Express.js shines when it comes to configuring different pieces of the puzzle; changing a template engine is a matter of a few lines of code.

The NPM userland provides tons of template engine choices—there are dozens of other template libraries that are easily compatible with Express.js, as you saw in the "Consolidate.js" section. They have different styles, design, and performances. For example, Swig, EJS, and some other libraries often outperform Jade in benchmark tests. And if you get used to the {{...}}} style of Handlebar and Mustache (e.g., from Angular.js)—or you don't have the time to learn Jade properly—then you can use those libraries right away!

This chapter concludes the configuration section of the app.js file. We move on to the routes. We'll start with the definition of routes and the extraction of parameters from URLs.

CHAPTER 4

■ ■ ■

Parameters and Routing

To review, the typical structure of an Express.js app (which is usually a `server.js` or `app.js` file) roughly consists of these parts, in the order shown:

1. Dependencies: A set of statements to import dependencies

2. Instantiations: A set of statements to create objects

3. Configurations: A set of statements to configure system and custom settings

4. Middleware: A set of statements that is executed for every incoming request

5. Routes: A set of statements that defines server routes, endpoints, and pages

6. Bootup: A set of statements that starts the server and makes it listen on a specific port for incoming requests

This chapter covers the fifth category, routes and the URL parameters that we define in routes. These parameters, along with the app.param() middleware, are essential because they allow the application to access information passed from the client in the URLs (e.g., books/proexpressjs). This is the most common convention for REST APIs. For example, the `http://hackhall.com/api/posts/521eb002d00c970200000003` route will use the value of 521eb002d00c970200000003 as the post ID.

Parameters are values passed in a query string of a URL of the request. If we didn't have Express.js or a similar library, and had to use just the core Node.js modules, we'd have to extract parameters from an `HTTP.request` (`http://nodejs.org/api/http.html#http_http_request_options_callback`) object via some `require('querystring').parse(url)` or `require('url').parse(url, true)` function "trickery."

Let's look closer at how to define a certain rule or logic for a particular URL parameter.

Parameters

The first approach to extracting parameters from the URLs is to write some code in the request handler (route). In case you need to repeat this snippet in other routes, you can abstract the code and manually apply the same logic to many routes. (To *abstract* code means to refactor the code so that it can be reused in other places and/or be organized better. This improves maintainability and readability of the code.)

For example, imagine that we need user information on a user profile page
(/v1/users/azat defined as /v1/users/:username) and on an admin page
(/v1/admin/azat defined as /v1/admin/:username). One way to do this is to define a
function that looks up the user information (findUserByUsername) and call this function
twice inside of each of the routes. This is how we can implement it (example ch4/app.js):

```
var users = {
  'azat': {
    email: 'hi@azat.co',
    website: 'http://azat.co',
    blog: 'http://webapplog.com'
  }
};

var findUserByUsername = function (username, callback) {
  // Perform database query that calls callback when it's done
  // This is our fake database
  if (!users[username])
    return callback(new Error(
      'No user matching '
      + username
      )
    );
  return callback(null, users[username]);
};

app.get('/v1/users/:username', function(request, response, next) {
  var username = request.params.username;
  findUserByUsername(username, function(error, user) {
    if (error) return next(error);
    return response.render('user', user);
  });
});

app.get('/v1/admin/:username', function(request, response, next) {
  var username = request.params.username;
  findUserByUsername(username, function(error, user) {
    if (error) return next(error);
    return response.render('admin', user);
  });
});
```

This example is also avalilable at https://github.com/azat-co/expressapiref/tree/master/ch4. You can run the app from the ch4 folder with $ node app command. Then, open a new terminal tab/window, and CURL a GET request with:

```
$ curl http://localhost:3000/v1/users/azat
```

To see this:

```
<h2>user profile</h2><p>http://azat.co</p><p>http://webapplog.com</p>
```

And with

```
$ curl http://localhost:3000/v1/admin/azat
```

To see this:

```
<h2>admin: user profile</h2><p>hi@azat.co</p><p>http://azat.co</p>
<p>http://webapplog.com</p><div><Practical>Node.js is your step-by-step
guide to learning how to build scalable real-world web applications, taking
you from installing Express.js to writing full-stack web applications with
powerful libraries such as Mongoskin, Everyauth, Mongoose, Socket.IO,
Handlebars, and everything in between.</Practical></div>
```

■ **Note** Windows users can download CURL from http://curl.haxx.se/download.html.

Alternatively, you can use the Postman Chrome extension at http://bit.ly/JGSQwr.

Or, for GET requests only, you can use your browser—just go to the URL. The browser won't make PUT or DELETE requests, and it will make POST requests only if you submit a form.

The last approach is to use jQuery to make AJAX/XHR requests, but be mindful about the cross-origin limitations, which means using the same domain, or CORS headers on the server. Or you could simply go to http://localhost:3000/v1/users/azat (see Figure 4-1) and http://localhost:3000/v1/admin/azat (see Figure 4-2) in your browser.

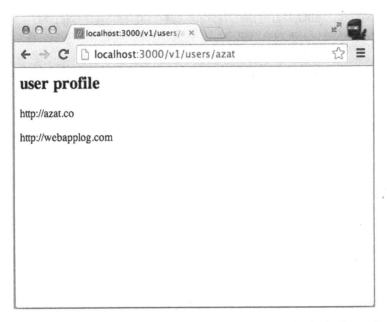

Figure 4-1. *Username URL parameter is parsed and used to find information displayed on the user page (example ch4)*

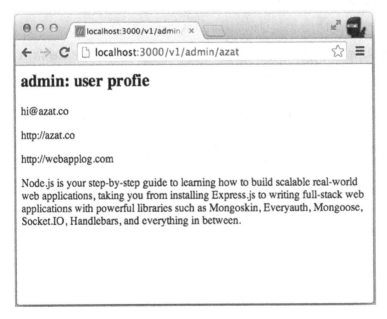

Figure 4-2. *Username URL parameter is parsed and used to find information displayed on the admin page (example ch4)*

The admin.jade template (Figure 4-2) has slightly different content from user.jade (Figure 4-1) to help you differentiate between the two pages/routes so you can be assured that both of them parse and use the parameters correctly.

Even after abstracting the bulk of the code into the findUserByUsername() function, we still ended up with ineloquent code. If we use the middleware approach, the code becomes a little bit better. The idea is to write a custom middleware findUserByUsernameMiddleware and use it with each route that needs the user information. Here's how you can refactor the same two routes and use the /v2 prefix (prefixes are usually used to differentiate REST API versions):

```
var findUserByUsername = function (username, callback) {
  // Perform database query that calls callback when it's done
  // This is our fake database!
  if (!users[username])
    return callback(new Error(
      'No user matching '
      + username
      )
    );
  return callback(null, users[username]);
};
var findUserByUsernameMiddleware = function(request, response, next){
  if (request.params.username) {
    console.log('Username param was detected: ', request.params.username)
    findUserByUsername(request.params.username, function(error, user){
      if (error) return next(error);
      request.user = user;
      return next();
    })
  } else {
    return next();
  }
}
// The v2 routes that use the custom middleware
app.get('/v2/users/:username',
  findUserByUsernameMiddleware,
  function(request, response, next){
  return response.render('user', request.user);
});
app.get('/v2/admin/:username',
  findUserByUsernameMiddleware,
  function(request, response, next){
  return response.render('admin', request.user);
});
```

The middleware findUserByUsernameMiddleware checks for the presence of the parameter (request.params.username) and then, if it's present, proceeds to fetch the information. This is a better pattern because it keeps routes lean and abstracts logic. However, Express.js has an even better solution. It's similar to the middleware method, but it makes our lives a bit easier by automatically performing the parameter presence checks (i.e., a check to see if the parameter is in the request). Meet the app.param() method!

app.param()

Anytime the given string (e.g., username) is present in the URL pattern of the route, and server receives a request that matches that route, the callback to the app.param() will be triggered. For example, with app.param('username', function(req, res, next, username){...}) and app.get('/users/:username', findUser) every time we have a request /username/azat or /username/tjholowaychuk, the closure in app.param() will be executed (before findUser).

The app.param() method is very similar to app.use() but it provides the value (username) in our example) as the fourth, last parameter, to the function. In this snippet, the username will have the value from the URL (e.g., 'azat' for /users/azat):

```
app.param('username', function (request, response, next, username) {
  // ... Perform database query and
  // ... Store the user object from the database in the req object
  req.user = user;
  return next();
});
```

No need of extra lines of code since we have req.user object populated by the app.param():

```
app.get('/users/:username', function(request, response, next) {
  //... Do something with req.user
  return res.render(req.user);
});
```

No need for extra code in this route either. We get req.user for free because of the app.param() defined earlier:

```
app.get('/admin/:username', function(request, response, next) {
  //... Same thing, req.user is available!
  return res.render(user);
});
```

Here is another example of how we can plug param middleware into our app:

```
app.param('id', function(request, response, next, id){
  // Do something with id
  // Store id or other info in req object
  // Call next when done
  next();
});

app.get('/api/v1/stories/:id', function(request, response){
  // Param middleware will be executed before and
  // We expect req objects to already have needed info
  // Output something
  res.send(data);
});
```

■ **Tip**   If you have a large application with many versions of API and routes (v1, v2, etc.), then it's better to use the `Router` class/object to organize the code of these routes. You create a `Router` object and mount it on a path, such as `/api` or `/api/v1`. Router is just a stripped-down version of the `var app = express()` object. More details about the `Router` class are provided later in the chapter.

The following is an example of plugging param middleware into an app that has a Mongoskin/Monk-like database connection in `req.db`:

```
app.param('id', function(request, response, next, id){
  req.db.get('stories').findOne({_id: id}, function (error, story){
    if (error) return next(error);
    if (!story) return next(new Error('Nothing is found'));
    req.story = story;
    next();
  });
});

app.get('/api/v1/stories/:id', function(request, response){
  res.send(req.story);
});
```

Or we can use multiple request handlers, but the concept remains the same: we can expect to have a req.story object or an error thrown prior to the execution of this code, so we abstract the common code/logic of getting parameters and their respective objects. Here is an example:

```
app.get('/api/v1/stories/:id', function(request, response, next) {
  //do authorization
  },
  //we have an object in req.story so no work is needed here
  function(request, response) {
    //output the result of the database search
    res.send(story);
});
```

▨ **Note**   Authorization and input sanitation are good candidates for residing in the middleware. For extensive examples of OAuth and Express.js, refer to *Practical Node.js*[1] (Apress, 2014).

The param() function is especially cool, because we can combine different variables in the routes; for example:

```
app.param('storyId', function(request, response, next, storyId) {
  // Fetch the story by its ID (storyId) from a database
  // Save the found story object into request object
  request.story = story;
});
app.param('elementId', function(request, response, next, elementId) {
  // Fetch the element by its ID (elementId) from a database
  // Narrow down the search when request.story is provided
  // Save the found element object into request object
  request.element = element;
});
app.get('/api/v1/stories/:storyId/elements/:elementId', function(request,
response){
  // Now we automatically get the story and element in the request object
  res.send({ story: request.story, element: request.element});
});
app.post('/api/v1/stories/:storyId/elements', function(request, response){
  // Now we automatically get the story in the request object
  // We use story ID to create a new element for that story
  res.send({ story: request.story, element: newElement});
});
```

---

[1]http://practicalnodebook.com

To summarize, by defining app.param once, its logic will be triggered for every route that has the matching URL parameter name. You might be wondering, "How is it different from writing your own function and calling it, or from writing your own custom middleware?" They will both execute the code properly, but param is a more elegant approach. We can refactor our earlier example to show the difference.

Let's go back to the ch4 project. If we refactor our previous example from ch4/app.js and use v3 as a new route prefix, we might end up with elegant code like this:

```
app.param('v3Username', function(request, response, next, username){
  console.log(
    'Username param was is detected: ',
    username
  )
  findUserByUsername(
    username,
    function(error, user){
      if (error) return next(error);
      request.user = user;
      return next();
    }
  );
});

app.get('/v3/users/:v3Username',
  function(request, response, next){
    return response.render('user', request.user);
  }
);
app.get('/v3/admin/:v3Username',
  function(request, response, next){
    return response.render('admin', request.user);
  }
);
```

So, extracting parameters is important, but defining routes is more important. Defining routes is also an alternative to using app.param() to extract values from URL parameters—this method is recommended when a parameter is used only once. If it's used more than once, param is a better pattern.

A lot of routes have already been defined in the three previous chapters. In the next section, we'll explore in more detail how to define various HTTP methods, chain middleware, abstract middleware code, and define all-method routes.

Routing

Express.js is a Node.js framework that, among other things, provides a way to organize routes into smaller subsections (Routers—instances of Router class/object). In Express.js 3.x and earlier, the only way to define routes is to use the app.VERB() pattern, which we'll cover next. However, starting with Express.js v4.x, using the new Router class is the *recommended* way to define routes, via router.route(path). We'll cover the traditional approach first.

app.VERB( )

Each route is defined via a method call on an application object with a URL pattern as the first parameter (regular expressions[2] are also supported); that is, app.METHOD(path, [callback...], callback).

For example, to define a GET /api/v1/stories endpoint:

```
app.get('/api/v1/stories/', function(request, response){
  // ...
})
```

Or, to define an endpoint for the POST HTTP method and the same route:

```
app.post('/api/v1/stories', function(request, response){
  // ...
})
```

DELETE, PUT, and other methods are supported as well. For more information, see http://expressjs.com/api.html#app.VERB.

The callbacks that we pass to get() or post() methods are called *request handlers* (covered in detail in Chapter 5), because they take requests (req), process them, and write to the response (res) objects. For example:

```
app.get('/about', function(request, response){
  res.send('About Us: ...');
});
```

We can have multiple request handlers in one route. All of them except the first and the last will be in the middle of the flow (order in which they are executed), hence the name *middleware*. They accept a third parameter/function, next, which when called (next()), switches the execution flow to the next handler. For example, we have three functions that perform authorization, database search and output:

```
app.get('/api/v1/stories/:id', function(request, response, next) {
  // Do authorization
  // If not authorized or there is an error
```

---

[2]http://en.wikipedia.org/wiki/Regular_expression

```
    // Return next(error);
    // If authorized and no errors
    return next();
}), function(request, response, next) {
    // Extract id and fetch the object from the database
    // Assuming no errors, save story in the request object
    request.story = story;
    return next();
}), function(request, response) {
    // Output the result of the database search
    res.send(response.story);
});
```

The name next() is an arbitrary convention, which means you can use anything else you like instead of next(). The Express.js uses the order of the arguments in the function to determine their meaning. The ID of a story is the URL parameter , which we need for finding matching items in the database.

Now, what if we have another route /admin. We can define multiple request handlers, which perform authentication, validation, and loading of resources:

```
app.get('/admin',
  function(request, response, next) {
    // Check active session, i.e.,
    // Make sure the request has cookies associated with a valid user session
    // Check if the user has administrator privileges
    return next();
  },  function(request, response, next){
    // Load the information required for admin dashboard
    // Such as user list, preferences, sensitive info
    return next();
  }, function(request, response) {
    // Render the information with proper templates
    // Finish response with a proper status
    res.end();
  })
```

But what if some of the code for /admin, such as authorization/authentication, is duplicated from the /stories? The following accomplishes the same thing, but is much *cleaner* with the use of named functions:

```
var auth = function (request, response, next) {
  // ... Authorization and authentication
  return next();
}
var getStory = function (request, response, next) {
  // ... Database request for story
  return next();
}
```

```
var getUsers = function (request, response, next) {
  // ... Database request for users
  return next();
}
var renderPage = function (request, response) {
  if (req.story) res.render('story', story);
  else if (req.users) res.render('users', users);
  else res.end();
}

app.get('/api/v1/stories/:id', auth, getStory, renderPage);
app.get('/admin', auth,  getUsers, renderPage);
```

Another useful technique is to pass callbacks as items of an array, made possible thanks to the inner workings of the arguments JavaScript mechanism:[3]

```
var authAdmin = function (request, response, next) {
  // ...
  return next();
}
var getUsers = function (request, response, next) {
  // ...
  return next();
}
var renderUsers = function (request, response) {
  // ...
  res.end();
}
var admin = [authAdmin, getUsers, renderUsers];
app.get('/admin', admin);
```

One distinct difference between request handlers in routes and middleware is that we can bypass the rest of the callbacks in the chain by calling next('route');. This might come in handy if, in the previous example with the /admin route, a request fails authentication in the first callback, in which case there's no need to proceed. You can also use next() to jump to the next route if you have multiple routes matching the same URL.

Please note that if the first parameter we pass to app.VERB() contains query strings (e.g., /?debug=true), that information is disregarded by Express.js. For example, app.get('/?debug=true', routes.index); will be treated exactly as app.get('/', routes.index);.

---

[3]See https://developer.mozilla.org/en-US/docs/Web/JavaScript/Reference/Functions_and_function_scope/arguments

The following are the most commonly used Representational State Transfer (REST) server architecture HTTP methods and their counterpart methods in Express.js along with the brief meaning:

- GET: app.get()—Retrieves an entity or a list of entities

- HEAD: app.head()–Same as GET, only without the body

- POST: app.post()—Submits a new entity

- PUT: app.put()—Updates an entity by complete replacement

- PATCH: app.patch()—Updates an entity partially

- DELETE: app.delete() and app.del()—Deletes an existing entity

- OPTIONS: app.options()—Retrieves the capabilities of the server

---

▨ **Tip** An HTTP method is a special property of every HTTP(S) request, similar to its headers or body. Opening a URL in your browser is a GET request, and submitting a form is a POST request. Other types of requests, such as PUT, DELETE, PATCH, and OPTIONS, are only available via special clients such as CURL, Postman, or custom-built applications (both front-end and back-end).

For more information on HTTP methods, please refer to RFC 2616 (http://tools.ietf.org/html/rfc2616) and its "Method Definitions" section (section 9).

app.all( )

The app.all() method allows the execution of specified request handlers on a particular path regardless of what the HTTP method of the request is. This procedure might be a lifesaver when defining *global* or namespace logic, as in this example:

```
app.all('*', userAuth);
...
app.all('/api/*', apiAuth);
```

Trailing Slashes

Paths with trailing slashes at the end are treated the same as their normal counterparts by default. To turn off this feature, use app.enable('strict routing'); or app. set('strict routing', true);. You can learn more about setting options in Chapter 1.

Router Class

The Router class is a mini Express.js application that has only middleware and routes. This is useful for abstracting certain modules based on the business logic that they perform. For example, all /users/* routes can be defined in one router, and all /posts/* routes can be defined in another. The benefit is that after we define a portion of the URL in the router with router.path() (see the next section), we don't need to repeat it over and over again, such as is the case with using the app.VERB() approach.

The following is an example of creating a router instance:

```
var express = require('express');
var router = express.Router(options);
// ... Define routes
app.use('/blog', router);
```

where options is an object that can have following properties:

- caseSensitive: Boolean indicating whether to treat routes with the same name but different letter case as different, false by default; e.g., if it's set to false, then /Users is the same as /users.

- strict: Boolean indicating whether to treat routes with the same name but with or without a trailing slash as different, false by default; e.g., if it's set to false, then /users is the same as /users/.

router.route(path)

The router.route(path) method is used to chain HTTP verb methods. For example, in a create, read, update, and delete (CRUD) server that has POST, GET, PUT, and DELETE endpoints for the /posts/:id URL (e.g., /posts/53fb401dc96c1caa7b78bbdb), we can use the Router class as follows:

```
var express = require('express');
var router = express.Router();
// ... Importations and configurations
router.param('postId', function(request, response, next) {
  // Find post by ID
  // Save post to request
  request.post = {
    name: 'PHP vs. Node.js',
    url: 'http://webapplog.com/php-vs-node-js'
  };
  return next();
});
```

```
router
  .route('/posts/:postId')
  .all(function(request, response, next){
    // This will be called for request with any HTTP method
  })
  .post(function(request, response, next){
  })
  .get(function(request, response, next){
    response.json(request.post);
  })
  .put(function(request, response, next){
    // ... Update the post
    response.json(request.post);
  })
  .delete(function(request, response, next){
    // ... Delete the post
    response.json({'message': 'ok'});
  })
```

The Router.route(path) method provides the convenience of chaining methods, which is a more appealing way to structure, your code than re-typing router for each route.

Alternatively, we can use router.VERB(path, [callback...], callback) to define the routes just as we would use app.VERB(). Similarly, the router.use() and router.param() methods work the same as app.use() and app.param().

Going back to our example project (in the ch4 folder), we can implement v4/users/:username and v4/admin/:username with Router:

```
router.param('username', function(request, response, next, username){
  console.log(
    'Username param was detected: ',
    username
  )
  findUserByUsername(
    username,
    function(error, user){
      if (error) return next(error);
      request.user = user;
      return next();
    }
  );
})
router.get('/users/:username',
  function(request, response, next){
    return response.render('user', request.user);
  }
);
```

```
router.get('/admin/:username',
  function(request, response, next){
    return response.render('admin', request.user);
  }
);
app.use('/v4', router);
```

As you can see, router.get() methods include no mention of v4. Typically, the router.get() and router.param() methods are abstracted into a separate file. This way, the main file (app.js in our example) stays lean and easy to read and maintain—a nice principle to follow!

Request Handlers

Request handlers in Express.js are strikingly similar to callbacks in the core Node.js http.createServer() method, because they're just functions (anonymous, named, or methods) with req and res parameters:

```
var ping = function(req, res) {
  console.log('ping');
  res.end(200);
};

app.get('/', ping);
```

In addition, we can utilize the third parameter, next(), for control flow. It's closely related to the topic of error handling, which is covered in Chapter 7. Here is a simple example of two request handlers, ping and pong where the former just skips to the latter after printing a word ping:

```
var ping = function(req, res, next) {
  console.log('ping');
  return next();
};
var pong = function(req, res) {
  console.log('pong');
  res.end(200);
};
app.get('/', ping, pong);
```

When a request comes on the / route, Express.js calls ping(), which acts as middleware in this case (because it's in the middle!). Ping, in turn, when it's done, calls pong with that finished response with res.end().

The return keyword is also very important. For example, we don't want to continue processing the request if the authentication has failed in the first middleware:

```
// Instantiate app and configure error handling

// Authentication middleware
var checkUserIsAdmin = function (req, res, next) {
  if (req.session && req.session._admin !== true) {
    return next (401);
  }
  return next();
};

// Admin route that fetches users and calls render function
var admin = {
  main: function (req, res, next) {
    req.db.get('users').find({}, function(e, users) {
      if (e) return next(e);
      if (!users) return next(new Error('No users to display.'));
      res.render('admin/index.html', users);
    });
  }
};

// Display list of users for admin dashboard
app.get('/admin', checkUserIsAdmin, admin.main);
```

The return keyword is essential, because if we don't use it for the next(e) call, the application will try to render (res.render()) even when there is an error and/or we don't have any users. For example, the following is probably a *bad idea* because after we call next(), which will trigger the appropriate error in the error handler, the flow goes on and tries to render the page:

```
var admin = {
  main: function (req, res, next) {
    req.db.get('users').find({}, function(e, users) {
      if (e) next(e);
      if (!users) next(new Error('No users to display.'));
      res.render('admin/index.html', users);
    });
  }
};
```

We should be using something like this:

```
if (!users) return next(new Error('No users to display.'));
res.render('admin/index.html', users);
```

or something like this:

```
if (!users)
  return next(new Error('No users to display.'));
else
  res.render('admin/index.html', users);
```

Summary

In this chapter we covered two major aspects of the typical structure of an Express.js app: defining routes and extracting URL parameters. We explored three different ways of how to get them out of the URL and use them in request handlers (req.params, custom middleware and app.param()). You learned how to define routes for various HTTP methods. Finally, we delved deep into the Router class, which acts as a mini Express.js application, and implemented yet another set of routes for the example project using the Router class.

Every time we defined a router (or a middleware), we used either an anonymous function definition or a named function in callbacks to define the request handler. The request handler usually has three parameters: request (or req), response (or res), and next. In the next chapter, you'll learn more about these objects, and how, in Express.js, they are different from the core Node.js http module's request and response. Knowing these differences will give you more features and functionality!

CHAPTER 5

■ ■ ■

Express.js Request Object

The Express.js request object (req for short) is a wrapper for a core Node.js http.request object which is the Node.js representation of the incoming HTTP(S) request. In web, the request has these parts:

- Method: GET, POST or others

- URI: the location for example http://hackhall.com/api/posts/

- Headers: host: www.hackhall.com

- Body: content in the urlencoded, JSON or other formats

The Express.js request object has some additional neat functionality, but essentially it supports everything that the native http.request object can do.

For example, Express.js automatically adds support for query parsing, which is essential when the system needs to access data in the URL in the following format (after the question mark): http://webapplog.com/?name1=value&name2=value.

Here the list of methods and objects of the Express.js request object that we'll cover in this chapter:

- request.query: query string parameters

- request.params: URL parameters

- request.body: request body data

- request.route: the route path

- request.cookies: cookie data

- request.signedCookies: signed cookie data

- request.header() and request.get(): request headers

■ **Tip** When you see request.*doSomething* in the code, don't confuse the Express.js request object with Mikeal Roger's request module (https://github.com/mikeal/request) or with the core Node.js http module's request (http://nodejs.org/api/http.html#http_event_request).

To better understand the request object, let's create a brand new Express.js app with Express.js version 4.8.1. This is the package.json file of the project (ch5/package.json):

```
{
  "name": "request",
  "version": "0.0.1",
  "private": true,
  "scripts": {
    "start": "node app.js"
  },
  "dependencies": {
    "express": "4.8.1",
    "errorhandler": "1.1.1",
    "jade": "1.5.0",
    "morgan": "1.2.2",
    "serve-favicon": "2.0.1",
    "cookie-parser": "1.3.2",
    "body-parser": "1.6.5",
    "debug": "~0.7.4",
    "serve-favicon": "2.0.1"
  }
}
```

Next we install the modules with NPM into our local project node_modules folder:

```
$ npm install
```

Now start the app with $ node app. It should display a standard Express.js Generator page with the text "Welcome to Express" (on http://localhost:3000). The full source code of app.js is provided for reference at the end of this chapter. You can download it from GitHub at https://github.com/azat-co/expressapiref.

request.query

The query string is everything to the right of the question mark in a given URL; for example, in the URL https://twitter.com/search?q=js&src=typd, the query string is q=js&src=typd. After the query string is parsed by Express.js, the resulting JS object would be {q:'js', src:'typd'}. This object is assigned to req.query or request. query in your request handler depending on what variable name you used in the function signature.

By default, the parsing is done by the qs module (http://npmjs.org/qs) which is used by Express.js behind the scenes via the express/lib/middleware/query.js internal module. This setting can be changed by the query parser setting, about which you learned in Chapter 1 (hopefully).

The way request.query works resembles body-parser's json() and cookie-parser middleware in that it puts a property (query in this case) on a request object req that is passed to the next middleware and routes. So without query parsing of some sort we can't access the request.query object. Again, Express.js uses qs parser by default—no extra code is needed on our part.

To illustrate request.query in an example, we can add a search route that will print the incoming search term in a query data format. The data is this example is q=js, q=nodejs, and q=nodejs&lang=fr. The server sends back JSON with the same query string data that we sent to it. We can add this route to any Express.js server, such as the one we've created with the CLI (i.e., ch5/request):

```
app.get('/search', function(req, res) {
  console.log(req.query)
  res.end(JSON.stringify(req.query)+'\r\n');
})
```

■ **Tip** The \n and \r are line feed and carriage return symbols, respectively, in ASCII and Unicode. They allow the text to start on a new line. For more information, please refer to http://en.wikipedia.org/wiki/Newline and http://en.wikipedia.org/wiki/Carriage_return.

Keep the server running ($ node app to start it), and in another terminal window, make the following GET requests with CURL:

```
$ curl -i "http://localhost:3000/search?q=js"
$ curl -i "http://localhost:3000/search?q=nodejs"
$ curl -i "http://localhost:3000/search?q=nodejs&lang=fr"
```

The result of CURL GET requests is shown in Figure 5-1, and the result of the server output is shown in Figure 5-2.

```
● ● ●                     📁 proexpressjs — bash
Azats-Air:proexpressjs azat$ curl "http://localhost:3000/search?q=js" -i
HTTP/1.1 200 OK
X-Powered-By: Express
Date: Tue, 26 Aug 2014 21:09:40 GMT
Connection: keep-alive
Transfer-Encoding: chunked

{"q":"js"}
Azats-Air:proexpressjs azat$ curl -i "http://localhost:3000/search?q=nodejs"
HTTP/1.1 200 OK
X-Powered-By: Express
Date: Tue, 26 Aug 2014 21:11:56 GMT
Connection: keep-alive
Transfer-Encoding: chunked

{"q":"nodejs"}
Azats-Air:proexpressjs azat$ curl -i "http://localhost:3000/search?q=nodejs&lang=fr"
HTTP/1.1 200 OK
X-Powered-By: Express
Date: Tue, 26 Aug 2014 21:12:07 GMT
Connection: keep-alive
Transfer-Encoding: chunked

{"q":"nodejs","lang":"fr"}
Azats-Air:proexpressjs azat$
```

Figure 5-1. Client-side results of running CURL commands with the query string parameters

```
● ● ●                        📁 ch7 — node
{ q: 'js' }
127.0.0.1 - - [Wed, 27 Aug 2014 14:23:09 GMT] "GET /search?q=js HTTP/1.1" 200 -
"-" "curl/7.30.0"
{ q: 'nodejs' }
127.0.0.1 - - [Wed, 27 Aug 2014 14:23:33 GMT] "GET /search?q=nodejs HTTP/1.1" 20
0 - "-" "curl/7.30.0"
{ q: 'nodejs', lang: 'fr' }
127.0.0.1 - - [Wed, 27 Aug 2014 14:23:49 GMT] "GET /search?q=nodejs&lang=fr HTTP
/1.1" 200 - "-" "curl/7.30.0"
```

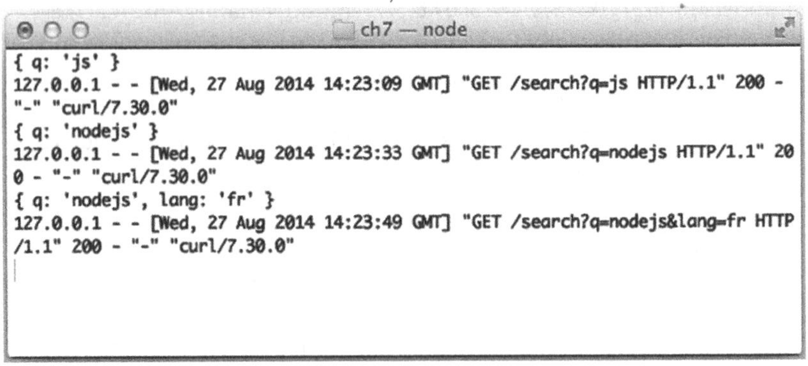

Figure 5-2. Server-side results of running CURL commands with the query string parameters

request.params

Chapter 4 covered how to set up middleware to process data taken from the URLs of the requests. However, sometimes it's more convenient just to get such values from within a specific request handler directly. For this, there's a request.params object, which is an array with key/value pairs.

To experiment with the request.params object, we can add a new route to our ch5/request application. This route will define URL parameters and print them in the console. Add the following route to request/app.js:

```
app.get('/params/:role/:name/:status', function(req, res) {
  console.log(req.params);
  res.end();
});
```

Next, run the following CURL terminal commands, as shown in Figure 5-3:

```
$ curl http://localhost:3000/params/admin/azat/active
$ curl http://localhost:3000/params/user/bob/active
```

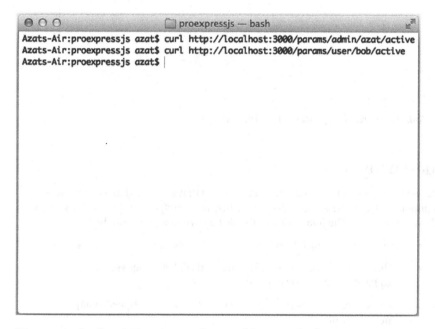

Figure 5-3. Sending GET requests with CURL (client window)

As shown in Figure 5-4, we see these server logs of the request.params object:

```
[ role: 'admin', name: 'azat', status: 'active' ]
[ role: 'user', name: 'bob', status: 'active' ]
```

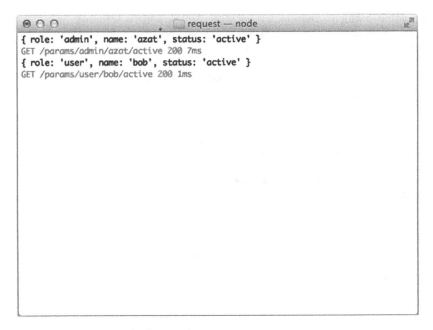

Figure 5-4. *Server result of processing request.params*

request.body

The request.body object is another magicical object that's provided to us by Express.
js. It's populated by applying the body-parser (express.bodyParser() in Express.js 3.x)
middleware functions. The body-parser module has two functions/middleware:

- json(): For parsing HTTP(S) payload into JavaScript/Node.js objects

- urlencoded(): For parsing URL-encoded HTTP(S) requests' data
  into JavaScript/Node.js objects

In both cases the resulting objects and data are put into the request.body
object—extremely convenient!

To use request.body, we need to install body-parser separately (if you're using ch5,
you can skip this step because the generator put it in package.json for us):

```
$ npm install body-parser@1.0.0
```

Then we need to import and apply it:

```
var bodyParser = require('body-parser');
// ...
app.use(bodyParser.json());
app.use(bodyParser.urlencoded());
```

You don't have to use both the json() and urlencoded() methods. Use only the one that is needed if that is sufficient.

To illustrate request.body in action, let's reuse our previous project and add the following route to see how the request.body object works, remembering that both bodyParser() middleware functions have been applied to the Express.js app already and are in the code:

```
app.post('/body', function(req, res){
  console.log(req.body);
  res.end(JSON.stringify(req.body)+'\r\n');
});
```

Again, submit a couple of HTTP POST requests with CURL or a similar tool:

```
$ curl http://localhost:3000/body -d 'name=azat'
$ curl -i http://localhost:3000/body -d 'name=azat&role=admin'
$ curl -i -H "Content-Type: application/json"
-d '{"username":"azat","password":"p@ss1"}' http://localhost:3000/body
```

■ **Tip** A brief CURL tip: The -H option sets headers, -d passes data, and -i enables verbose logging.

The preceding commands yield request.body objects as you can see in the client terminal in Figure 5-5 and in the server terminal in Figure 5-6:

```
{ name: 'azat' }
{ name: 'azat', role: 'admin' }
{ username: 'azat', password: 'p@ss1' }
```

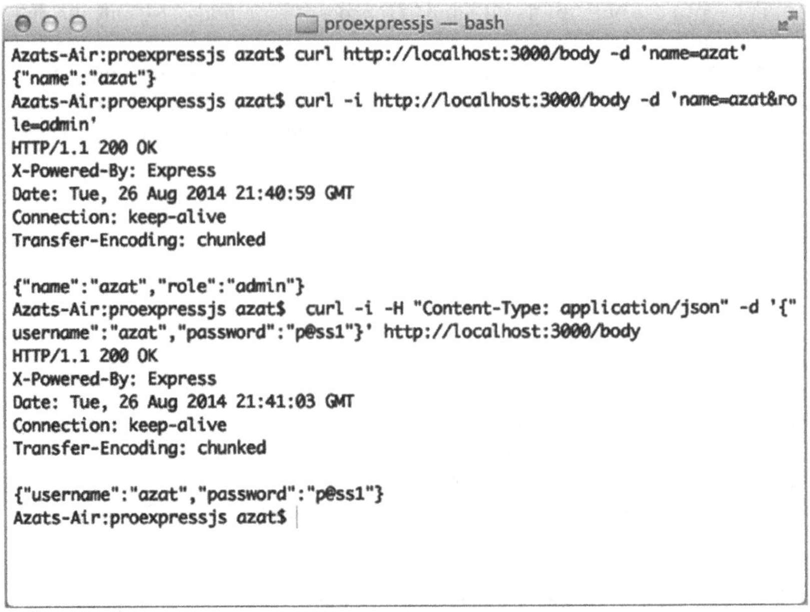

```
● ○ ○                    📁 proexpressjs — bash                          ⬚
Azats-Air:proexpressjs azat$ curl http://localhost:3000/body -d 'name=azat'
{"name":"azat"}
Azats-Air:proexpressjs azat$ curl -i http://localhost:3000/body -d 'name=azat&ro
le=admin'
HTTP/1.1 200 OK
X-Powered-By: Express
Date: Tue, 26 Aug 2014 21:40:59 GMT
Connection: keep-alive
Transfer-Encoding: chunked

{"name":"azat","role":"admin"}
Azats-Air:proexpressjs azat$  curl -i -H "Content-Type: application/json" -d '{"
username":"azat","password":"p@ss1"}' http://localhost:3000/body
HTTP/1.1 200 OK
X-Powered-By: Express
Date: Tue, 26 Aug 2014 21:41:03 GMT
Connection: keep-alive
Transfer-Encoding: chunked

{"username":"azat","password":"p@ss1"}
Azats-Air:proexpressjs azat$ |
```

Figure 5-5. *Sending POST requests with CURL (client logs)*

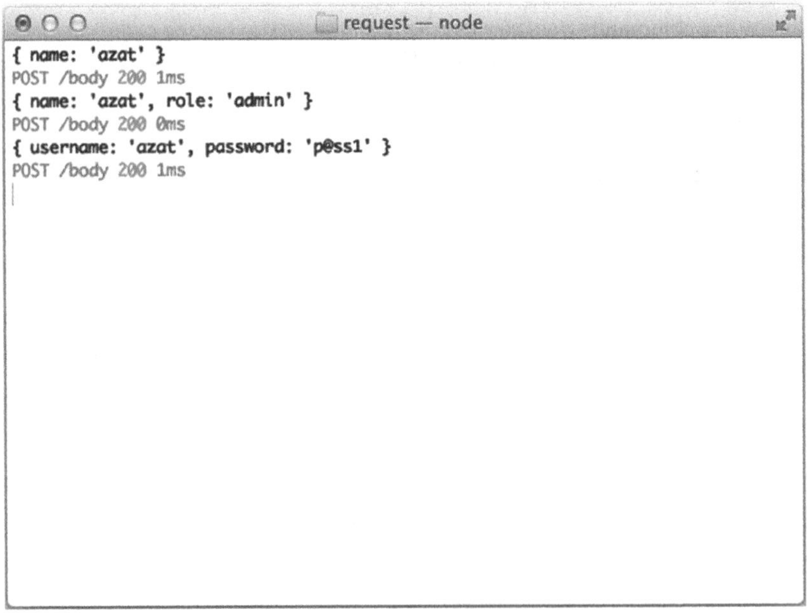

```
● ○ ○                    📁 request — node                              ⬚
{ name: 'azat' }
POST /body 200 1ms
{ name: 'azat', role: 'admin' }
POST /body 200 0ms
{ username: 'azat', password: 'p@ss1' }
POST /body 200 1ms
|
```

Figure 5-6. *Result of processing request.body (server logs)*

request.route

The request.route object simply has the current route's information, such as:

- path: Original URL pattern of the request
- method: HTTP method of the request
- keys: List of parameters in the URL pattern (i.e., values prefixed with :)
- regexp: Express.js-generated pattern for the path
- params: request.params object

We can add the console.log(request.route); statement to our request.params route from the example in the previous section like this:

```
app.get('/params/:role/:name/:status', function(req, res) {
  console.log(req.params);
  console.log(req.route);
  res.end();
});
```

Then, if we send the HTTP GET request

```
$ curl http://localhost:3000/params/admin/azat/active
```

we should get the server logs of the request.route object, which has path, stack, and methods properties:

```
{ path: '/params/:role/:name/:status',
  stack: [ { method: 'get', handle: [Function] } ],
  methods: { get: true } }
```

The request.route object might be useful when used from within middleware—that is, used on multiple routes—to find out which route is currently used.

request.cookies

The cookie-parser (formerly express.cookieParser() in Express.js 3.x and earlier) middleware (https://www.npmjs.org/package/cookie-parser, https://github.com/expressjs/cookie-parser) allows us to access requests' cookies in a JavaScript/Node. js format. The cookie-parser is required for express-session middleware, because web sessions work by storing their session ID in the browser cookies.

With cookie-parser installed (with NPM), imported (with require()), and applied (with app.use()), we get access to the HTTP(S) request cookies (user-agent cookies) via the request.cookies object. Cookies are automatically presented as a JavaScript object; for example, you can extract the session ID with:

```
request.cookies['connect.sid']
```

■ **Caution**   Storing sensitive information in browser cookies is discouraged because of security concerns. Also, some browsers impose a limitation on the size of a cookie, which might lead to bugs (Internet Explorer!). I usually use `request.cookie` only for the `request.session` support.

■ **Note**   Refer to Chapter 2 for more information on how to install and apply middleware.

The cookie info can be stored using `response.cookie()` or `res.cookie()`. The Express.js response object is covered in Chapter 6. To illustrate `request.cookies`, we can implement a `/cookies` route that will increment a counter, change the value of a cookie, and display the result on a page. This is the code that you can add to `ch5/request`:

```
app.get('/cookies', function(req, res){
  if (!req.cookies.counter)
    res.cookie('counter', 0);
  else
    res.cookie('counter', parseInt(req.cookies.counter,10) + 1);
  res.status(200).send('cookies are: ', req.cookies);
})
```

■ **Tip**   The `parseInt()` method is needed to prevent JavaScript/Node.js from treating the number value as a string, which would result in 0, 01, 011, 0111, etc. instead of 0, 1, 2, 3, etc. Using `parseInt()` with the radix/base (second argument) is recommended to prevent numbers from being converted wrongly.

As a result of going to `http://localhost:3000/cookies` and refreshing it a few times, you should see the counter increment from 0 up, as shown in Figure 5-7.

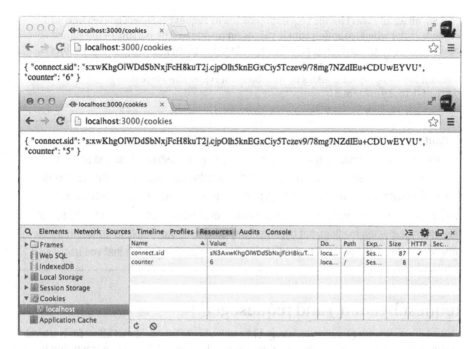

Figure 5-7. *Cookie value is saved in the browser and incremented by the server on each request*

Inspection of the Network or Resource tab in Chrome Developer Tools will reveal the presence of a cookie with the name `connect.sid` (see Figure 5-7). The cookies are shared between browser windows, so even if we open a new window, the counter will increment by 1 from the value in the original window.

request.signedCookies

`request.signedCookies` is akin to `request.cookies`, but it's used when the secret string is passed to the `express.cookieParser('some secret string');` method. To populate `request.signedCookies`, you can use `response.cookie` with the flag `signed: true`. Here's how we can modify our previous route to switch to signed cookies:

```
app.use(cookieParser('abc'));
// ... Other middleware
app.get('/signed-cookies', function(req, res){
  if (!req.signedCookies.counter)
    res.cookie('counter', 0, {signed: true});
  else
    res.cookie('counter', parseInt(req.signedCookies.counter,10) + 1,
{signed: true});
  res.status(200).send('cookies are: ', req.signedCookies);
});
// ... Server boot-up
```

So, all we did was change request.cookies to request.signedCookies and add signed: true when assigning cookie values on response. The parsing of the signed cookies is done automatically, and they are placed in plain JavaScript/Node.js objects. Note that 'abc' is an arbitrary string. You can use $ uuidgen on Mac OS X to generate a random key to sign your cookies or web-based services like Random.org (http://bit.ly/1F1fbL8).

■ **Caution** Signing a cookie *does not* hide or encrypt the cookie. It's a simple way to prevent tampering by applying a private value. Signing (or hashing) is not the same as encryption. The former is for identification and tampering prevention, and the latter is for hiding the content from unauthorized recipients (see, e.g., http://danielmiessler.com/study/encoding_encryption_hashing). You can encrypt your cookie data on the server (and decrypt it when reading), but hypothetically this is still vulnerable to brute-force attacks. The level of vulnerability depends on the encryption algorithm that you use.

---

request.header( ) and request.get( )

The request.header() and request.get() methods are identical and allow for retrieval of the HTTP(S) requests' headers by their names. Fortunately, the header naming is case insensitive:

```
request.get('Content-Type');
request.get('content-type');
request.header('content-type');
```

Other Attributes and Methods

We've covered the most commonly used and most important methods and objects of the Express.js request object. They should suffice in the majority of cases. But the list doesn't stop there. For convenience, there are plenty of *sugar-coating* objects in the Express.js request (see Table 5-1). Sugar-coating means that most of the functions of these objects can be implemented with the foundational methods, but they are more eloquent than the foundational methods. For example, the request.accepts can be replaced with if/else and request.get(), which gives us request headers. Of course, if you understand these methods, you can use them to make your code more elegant and easier to read.

Table 5-1. *Other Attributes and Methods in the Express.js Request*

Attribute/Method	Conditions/Definition	API
request.accepts()	true if a passed string (single or comma-separated values) or an array of MIME types (or extensions) matches the request Accept header; false if there's no match	http://expressjs.com/api.html#req.accepts
request.accepted	An array of accepted MIME types	http://expressjs.com/api.html#req.accepted
request.is()	true if a passed MIME type string matches the Content-Type header types; false if there's no match	http://expressjs.com/api.html#req.is
request.ip	The IP address of the request; see trust proxy configuration in Chapter 1	http://expressjs.com/api.html#req.ip
request.ips	An array of IPs when trust proxy configuration is enabled	http://expressjs.com/api.html#req.ips
request.path	String with a URL path of the request	http://expressjs.com/api.html#req.path
request.host	Value from the Host header of the request	http://expressjs.com/api.html#req.host
request.fresh	true if request is *fresh* based on Last-Modified and ETag headers; false otherwise	http://expressjs.com/api.html#req.fresh
request.stale	Opposite of req.fresh	http://expressjs.com/api.html#req.stale
request.xhr	true if the request is an AJAX call via X-Requested-With header and its XMLHttpRequest value	http://expressjs.com/api.html#req.xhr
request.protocol	Request protocol value (e.g., http or https)	http://expressjs.com/api.html#req.protocol
request.secure	true if the request protocol is https	http://expressjs.com/api.html#req.secure
request.subdomains	Array of subdomains from the Host header	http://expressjs.com/api.html#req.subdomains
request.originalUrl	Unchangeable value of the request URL	http://expressjs.com/api.html#req.originalUrl

(continued)

93

Table 5-1. *(continued)*

Attribute/Method	Conditions/Definition	API
request. acceptedLanguages	Array of language code (e.g., en-us, en) from the request's Accept-Language header	http://expressjs. com/api.html#req. acceptedLanguages
request. acceptsLanguage()	true if a passed language code is in the request header	http://expressjs. com/api.html#req. acceptsLanguage
request. acceptedCharsets	Array of charsets (e.g., iso-8859-5) from the request's Accept-Charset header	http://expressjs. com/api.html#req. acceptedCharsets
request. acceptsCharset()	true if a passed charset is in the request header	http://expressjs. com/api.html#req. acceptsCharset

We've been making small adjustments to the ch5 project throughout this chapter, so now it's time to see the whole picture. Therefore, here's the full source code of the final request server from the ch5/app.js file (available at https://github.com/azat-co/expressapiref):

```
var express = require('express');
var path = require('path');
var favicon = require('serve-favicon');
var logger = require('morgan');
var cookieParser = require('cookie-parser');
var bodyParser = require('body-parser');

var routes = require('./routes/index');

var app = express();

// View engine setup
app.set('views', path.join(__dirname, 'views'));
app.set('view engine', 'jade');
app.use(logger('combined'));
app.use(favicon(path.join(__dirname, 'public', 'favicon.ico')));
app.use(bodyParser.json());
app.use(bodyParser.urlencoded({extended: true}));
app.use(cookieParser('abc'));
app.use(express.static(path.join(__dirname, 'public')));
```

```
app.use('/', routes);

app.get('/search', function(req, res) {
  console.log(req.query);
  res.end(JSON.stringify(req.query)+'\r\n');
});

app.get('/params/:role/:name/:status', function(req, res) {
  console.log(req.params);
  console.log(req.route);
  res.end();
});

app.post('/body', function(req, res){
  console.log(req.body);
  res.end(JSON.stringify(req.body)+'\r\n');
});

app.get('/cookies', function(req, res){
  if (!req.cookies.counter)
    res.cookie('counter', 0);
  else
    res.cookie('counter', parseInt(req.cookies.counter,10) + 1);
  res.status(200).send('cookies are: ', req.cookies);
});

app.get('/signed-cookies', function(req, res){
  if (!req.signedCookies.counter)
    res.cookie('counter', 0, {signed: true});
  else
    res.cookie('counter', parseInt(req.signedCookies.counter,10) + 1,
{signed: true});
  res.status(200).send('cookies are: ', req.signedCookies);
});

/// Catch 404 and forward to error handler
app.use(function(req, res, next) {
    var err = new Error('Not Found');
    err.status = 404;
    next(err);
});

/// Error handlers
```

```
// Development error handler
// Will print stacktrace
if (app.get('env') === 'development') {
    app.use(function(err, req, res, next) {
        res.status(err.status || 500);
        res.render('error', {
            message: err.message,
            error: err
        });
    });
}

// Production error handler
// No stacktraces leaked to user
app.use(function(err, req, res, next) {
    res.status(err.status || 500);
    res.render('error', {
        message: err.message,
        error: {}
    });
});

module.exports = app;

var debug = require('debug')('request');

app.set('port', process.env.PORT || 3000);

var server = app.listen(app.get('port'), function() {
  debug('Express server listening on port ' + server.address().port);
});
```

Summary

Understanding and working with HTTP requests is at the foundation of web development. The way in which Express.js approaches requests is by adding objects and properties. Developers use them inside of the request handlers. Express.js provides many objects and methods in the request, and in areas where it does not, there are plenty of third-party options.

In the next chapter we'll cover the Express.js response. The response object is the counterpart of the request object. Response is the stuff that we actually send back to the client. Similar to request, the Express.js response object has special methods and objects as its properties. We'll cover the most important and then list the rest of the built-in properties.

CHAPTER 6

Response

The Express.js response object (res for short)—which is an argument in the request handler callbacks—is the same good old Node.js http.response object[1] on steroids. This is because the Express.js response object has new methods. In other words, the Express.js response object is the extension of the http.response class.

Why would some use these additional methods? Indeed, you can use the response.end() method[2] and other core methods, but then you'll have to do write more code. For example, you would have to add Content-Type header manually. But with the Express.js response object which contains convenient wrappers, such as response.json() and response.send(), appropriate Content-Type is added automatically.

In this chapter, we'll cover the following methods and attributes of the Express.js response object in great details:

- response.render()
- response.locals
- response.set()
- response.status()
- response.send()
- response.json()
- response.jsonp()
- response.redirect()

To demonstrate these methods in action, they are used in the kitchen-sink app ch6/app.js. The code is also available at https://github.com/azat-co/expressapiref/tree/master/ch6. Other methods and properties along with their meanings will be listed in the Table 8-1. At the end of the chapter, we'll cover how to work with streams and Express.js response.

---

[1]http://nodejs.org/api/http.html#http_class_http_serverresponse.
[2]http://nodejs.org/api/http.html#http_response_end_data_encoding.

To start with the example app, create a brand new Express.js app with express-generator and the $ express response terminal command. Obviously, now you need to run $ cd response && npm install to download the dependencies. The initial ch6/app.js app will be identical to the initial app from Chapter 5.

response.render()

The response.render() method is the staple of Express.js. From our previous examples and from the function's name, you could guess that it has something to do with generating HTML out of templates (such as Jade, Handlebars, or EJS) and data.

The response.render(name, [data,] [callback]) method takes three parameters, but only one is mandatory and it's the first parameter: name, which is the template name in a string format. The other parameters are data and callback. If you omit data but have callback, then callback becomes the number two argument.

The template name can be identified with or without an extension. For more information on template engine extensions, please refer to Chapter 3.

To illustrate the most straightforward use case for response.render(), we'll create a page that shows a heading and a paragraph from a Jade template.

First, add a route. Here is an example of a simple setup for the home page route in the response/app.js file:

```
app.get('/render', function(req, res) {
  res.render('render');
});
```

Then, add a new views/render.jade file that looks static for now (i.e., it has no variables or logic):

```
extends layout

block content
  h1= 'Pro Express.js'
  p Welcome to the Pro Express.js Response example!
```

Finally, start the response application with $ node app and go to http://localhost:3000 in a browser. You should see the welcome message shown in Figure 6-1.

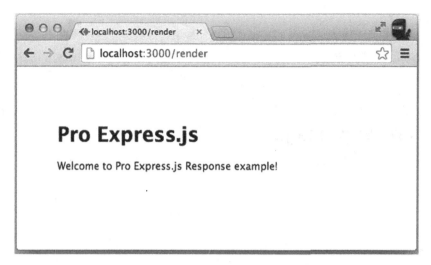

Figure 6-1. The result of plain response.render() call without parameters

---

■ **Note**   Jade uses Python/Haml-like syntax, which takes into account whitespace and tabs—be careful with the markup. We can use = as a *print* command (h1 tag) or nothing (p tag). For more information, please visit the official documentation (http://jade-lang.com/) or check out *Practical Node.js* (Apress, 2014)[3].

In addition to the mandatory name parameter, response.render(), has two optional parameters, data and callback. The data parameter makes templates more dynamic than static HTML files, and allows us to update the output. For example, we can pass title to overwrite the value in the default value:

```
app.get('/render-title', function(req, res) {
  res.render('index', {title: 'Pro Express.js'});
});
```

The index.jade file remains the same. It prints the title value, and looks like this:

```
extends layout

block content
  h1= title
  p Welcome to #{title}
```

The result of the /render-title route is shown in Figure 6-2. The h1 title text has changed to Pro Express.js.

---

[3]http://practicalnodebook.com.

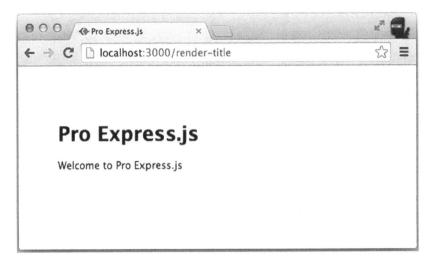

Figure 6-2. *The response.render() example with the data parameter that has a title property*

The `response.render()` callback parameter accepts two parameters itself: `error` and `html` (an HTML string which is the output). This example is not in the `res/app.js` project, but shows how to pass callbacks to `response.render()`:

```
app.get('/render-title', function(req, res) {
  res.render('index', {title: 'Pro Express.js'}, function (error, html) {
    // Do something
  });
});
```

■ **Caution** The properties of the `data` parameter are your locals in the template. In other words, if you want to access a value of a title inside of your template, the data object must contain a key/value pair. Nested objects are supported by most of the template engines.

The `callback` can take the place of the `data` because Express.js is able to determine the type of the parameter. This example is not within `response/app.js` but shows how to pass callbacks with our data:

```
app.get('/render-title', function(req, res) {
  res.render('index', function (error, html) {
    // Do something
  });
});
```

Behind the scenes, response.render() calls response.send() (which is covered later in this chapter) for successful compilation of HTML strings or calls req.next(error) for failure, *if the callback is not provided*. In other words, the default callback to response. render() is code from the version 3.3.5 location on GitHub at https://github.com/visionmedia/express/blob/3.3.5/lib/response.js#L753:

```
// Default callback to respond
fn = fn || function(err, str){
  if (err) return req.next(err);
  self.send(str);
};
```

Looking at this code, you can see that it's easy to write your own callback to do just about anything as long as there's an ending to the response (response.json, response. send, or response.end).

response.locals

The response.locals object is another way to pass data to the templates so that both the data and the template can be compiled into HTML. You already know that the first way is to pass data as a parameter to the response.render() method, as previously outlined:

```
app.get('/render-title', function(req, res) {
  res.render('index', {title: Pro Express.js'});
});
```

However, with response.locals, we can achieve the same thing. Our object will be available inside of the template:

```
app.get('/locals', function(req, res){
  res.locals = { title: 'Pro Express.js' };
  res.render('index');
});
```

Again, the index.jade Jade template remains the same:

```
extends layout

block content
  h1= title
  p Welcome to #{title}
```

You can see the web page that has the Pro Express.js title in Figure 6-3. But if nothing has changed, then what is a benefit of `response.locals`? The advantage is that we can expose (i.e., pass to templates) info in one middleware, but render the actual template later in another request handler. For example, you can perform authentication without rendering (this code is not in the `ch6/app.js`):

```
app.get('/locals',
  function(req, res){
    res.locals = { user: {admin: true}};
    next();
  }, function(req, res){
    res.render('index');
});
```

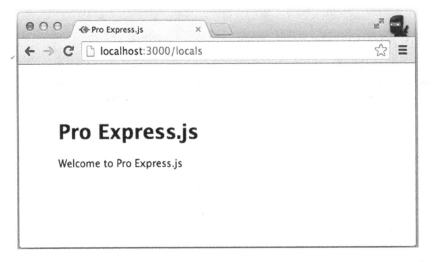

Figure 6-3. *The response.locals example renders the same page as the response.render() example*

■ **Tip** Sometimes for debugging it's useful to see a list of all the variables available in a particular Jade template. To do so, simply insert this log statement: - `console.log(locals);`. For more information on Jade, please refer to *Practical Node.js* (Apress, 2014)[4].

---

[4]http://practicalnodebook.com.

response.set( )

The response.set(field, [value]) method is an alias of response.header() (or the other way around) and serves as a wrapper for the Node.js http core module's response. setHeader() function[5]. The main difference is that Express.js' response.set() is smart enough to call itself recursively when we pass multiple header-value pairs to it in the form of an object. See the CSV example later in this section if the previous sentence didn't make much sense to you.

Here is an example from ch6/app.js of setting a single Content-Type response header to text/html and then sending some simple HTML to the client:

```
app.get('/set-html', function(req, res) {
  // Some code
  res.set('Content-Type', 'text/html');
  res.end('<html><body>' +
    '<h1>Express.js Guide</h1>' +
    '</body></html>');
});
```

You can see the results in the Network tab of Chrome Developer Tools, under the Headers subtab, which says Content-Type: text/html (see Figure 6-4). If we didn't have response.set() with text/html, then the response would still have the HTML but *without the header*. Feel free to comment the response.set() and see it for yourself.

---

[5]http://nodejs.org/api/http.html#http_response_setheader_name_value.

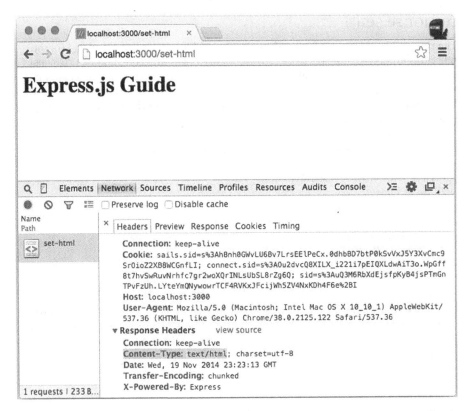

Figure 6-4. *The response.set() example rendering HTML with the Content-Type: text/html header*

The Content-Type disappears when we don't set it explicitly with `response.set()`, because Express.js' `response.send()` automatically adds `Content-Type` and other headers, but core `response.end()` does not. More on `response.send()` later in this chapter.

Often though, our servers need to provide more than one header so that all the different browsers and other HTTP clients process it properly. Let's explore an example of passing multiple values to the `response.set()` method.

Imagine that the service we are building sends out comma-separated value (CVS) files with books' titles and their tags. This is how we can implement this route in the `ch6/app.js` file:

```
app.get('/set-csv', function(req, res) {
  var body = 'title, tags\n' +
    'Practical Node.js, node.js express.js\n' +
    'Rapid Prototyping with JS, backbone.js node.js mongodb\n' +
    'JavaScript: The Good Parts, javascript\n';
```

```
res.set({'Content-Type': 'text/csv',
  'Content-Length': body.length,
  'Set-Cookie': ['type=reader', 'language=javascript']});
res.end(body);
});
```

Now if you steer Chrome to http://localhost:3000/set-csv, the browser will recognize the CSV MIME type and download the file instead of opening it (at least with the default Chrome settings and without extra extensions). You can see the headers in Figure 6-5.

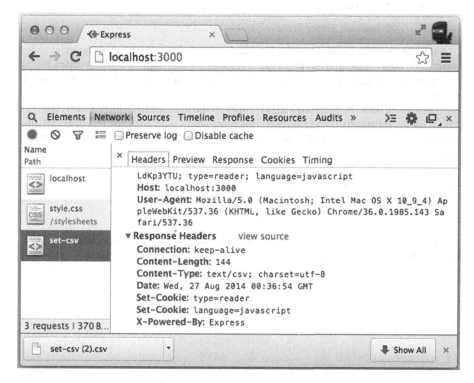

Figure 6-5. The response.set() example rendering Content-Length, Content-Type, and Set-Cookie headers with CSV data

response.status()

The response.status() method accepts an HTTP status code[6] number and sends it in response. The most common HTTP status codes are:

- 200: OK

- 201: Created

- 301: Moved Permanently

- 401: Unauthorized

- 404: Not Found

- 500: Internal Server Error

You can find a lengthier list of HTTP statuses in Chapter 7. The only difference between its core counterpart[7] is that response.status() is chainable. Status codes are important for building REST APIs because they enable you to standardize the outcome of the request.

Let's demo how response.status() works on the pulse route, which returns 200 (OK) if the server is still up and running. This route won't send back any text or HTML on purpose. We use response.end() because response.send() will automatically add the proper status code 200:

```
app.get('/status', function(req, res) {
  res.status(200).end();
});
```

If you go to http://localhost:3000/status, you'll see a green circle and the number 200, as shown in Figure 6-6.

---

[6]http://www.w3.org/Protocols/rfc2616/rfc2616-sec10.html.
[7]http://nodejs.org/api/http.html#http_response_statuscode.

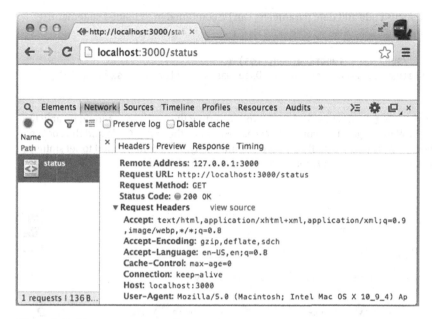

Figure 6-6. The response.status() example response

response.send()

The response.send() method lies somewhere between high-level response.render()
and low-level response.end(). The response.send() method conveniently outputs any
data application thrown at it (such as strings, JavaScript objects, and even Buffers)
with automatically generated *proper* HTTP headers (e.g., Content-Length, ETag, or
Cache-Control).

Due to its omnivorous (consumes any input) behavior (caused by arguments.
length), response.send() can be used in countless ways with these input parameters:

- *String*: response.send('success'); with text/html

- *Object*: response.send({message: 'success'}); or response.
  send({message: 'error'}); with JSON representation

- *Array*: response.send([{title: 'Practical Node.js'},
  {title: 'Rapid Prototyping with JS'}]); with JSON
  representation

- *Buffer*: response.send(new Buffer('Express.js Guide'));
  with application/octet-stream

■ **Tip** Sending numbers with response.send(number) as a status code is deprecated in
Express.js 4.x. Use response.status(number).send() instead.

107

The status code and data parameters can be combined in a chained statement; for example:

```
app.get('/send-ok', function(req, res) {
  res.status(200).send({message: 'Data was submitted successfully.'});
});
```

After adding the new send-ok route and restarting the server, you should be able to see the JSON message when you go to /send-ok. Notice the Status Code and the Content-Type header. Although 200 will be added automatically, it's recommended to set statuses for all other cases, such as 201 for Created or 404 for Not Found.

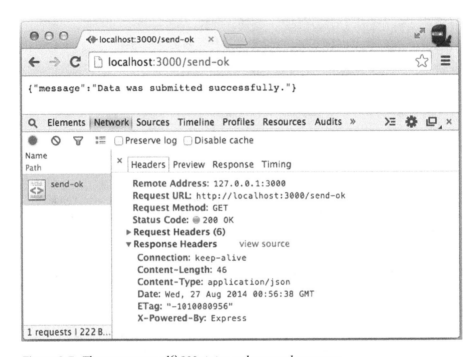

Figure 6-7. *The response.send() 200 status code example response*

The following is an example of sending the 500 Internal Server Error status code along with the error message (used for server errors):

```
app.get('/send-err', function(req, res) {
  res.status(500).send({message: 'Oops, the server is down.'});
});
```

Again, when you check this route in the browser, there's a JSON content type but now you see a red circle and the number 500.

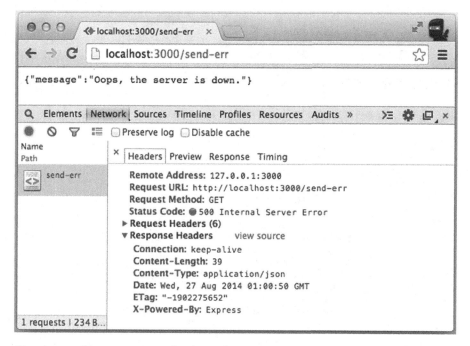

Figure 6-8. The response.status(500).send() 500 status code example response

The headers generated by `response.send()` might be overwritten if specified explicitly before. For example, the Buffer type will have `Content-Type` as `application/octet-stream`, but we can change it to `text/plain` with

```
app.get('/send-buf', function(req, res) {
  res.set('Content-Type', 'text/plain');
  res.send(new Buffer('text data that will be converted into Buffer'));
});
```

The resulting content type and text are shown in Figure 6-9.

109

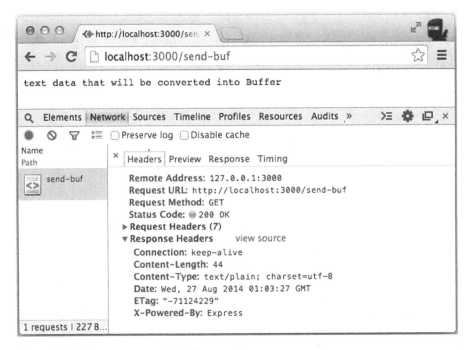

Figure 6-9. *The response.send() Buffer example response*

■ **Note** Virtually all core Node.js methods (and Connect.js methods as well) are available in Express.js objects. Therefore, we have access to `response.end()` and other methods in the Express.js response API.

---

response.json()

The `response.json()` method is a convenient way of sending JSON data. It's equivalent to `response.send()` when data passed is Array or Object type. In other cases, `response.json()` forces data conversion with `JSON.stringify()`. By default, the header `Content-Type` is set to `application/json`, but can be overwritten prior to `response.json()` with `response.set()`.

If you remember our old friends from Chapter 1, `json replacer` and `json spaces`, that's where these settings are taken into account (i.e., used).

The most common use of response.json() is with appropriate status codes:

```
app.get('/json', function(req, res) {
  res.status(200).json([{title: 'Practical Node.js', tags: 'node.js express.js'},
    {title: 'Rapid Prototyping with JS', tags: 'backbone.js node.js mongodb'},
    {title: 'JavaScript: The Good Parts', tags: 'javascript'}
  ]);
});
```

Please note the JSON Content-Type and Content-Length headers produced by response.json() in Figure 6-10.

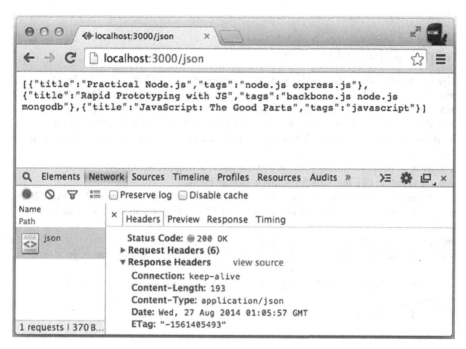

Figure 6-10. *The result of using response.json(): automatically generated headers*

■ **Note**   The screenshot of the response.json() example in Figure 6-10 was taken after adding the route to the ch6/app.js file of the ch6/app.js project. You are encouraged to try doing this on your own.

Other uses of response.json() are possible as well— for example, with no status code:

```
app.get('/api/v1/stories/:id', function(req,res){
  res.json(req.story);
});
```

Assuming req.story is an array or an object, the following code would produce similar results as the preceding snippet (no need to set the header to application/json in either case):

```
app.get('/api/v1/stories/:id', function(req,res){
  res.send(req.story);
});
```

response.jsonp()

The response.jsonp() method is similar to response.json() but provides a JSONP response. That is, the JSON data is wrapped in a JavaScript function call; for example, processResponse({...});. This is usually used for cross-domain calls support. By default, Express.js uses a callback name to extract the name of the callback function. It's possible to override this value with jsonp callback name settings (more about it in Chapter 1).

If there is no proper callback specified in the query string of the request (e.g., ?callback=cb), then the response is simply JSON.

Assume that we need to serve CSV data to a front-end request via JSONP (status(200) is optional, because Express will automatically add the proper status of 200 by default):

```
app.get('/', function (req, res) {
  res.status(200).jsonp([{title: 'Express.js Guide', tags: 'node.js express.
js'},
    {title: 'Rapid Prototyping with JS', tags: 'backbone.js, node.js,
mongodb'},
    {title: 'JavaScript: The Good Parts', tags: 'javascript'}
  ]);
});
```

■ **Note**   The screenshot of the response.json() example in Figure 6-11 was taken after adding the route to the index.js file of the ch2/cli-app/app.js project. You are encouraged to try doing this on your own.

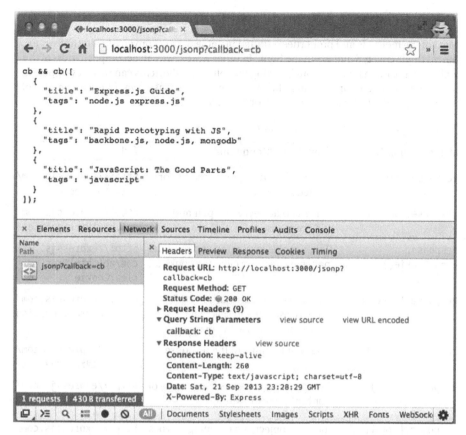

Figure 6-11. *The result of response.jsonp() and ?callback=cb is a text/javascript header and JavaScript function prefix*

response.redirect()

Sometimes we simply need to redirect users/requests to another route. We can use absolute, relative, or full paths:

```
res.redirect('/admin');
res.redirect('../users');
res.redirect('http://rapidprototypingwithjs.com');
```

By default, `response.redirect()` sends the 302 (Found/Temporarily Moved) status code[8]. Of course, we can configure it to our liking in the same manner as `response.send()`; that is, pass the first status code number as the first parameter (301 is Moved Permanently):

```
res.redirect(301, 'http://rpjs.co');
```

---

[8]http://www.w3.org/Protocols/rfc2616/rfc2616-sec10.html.

Other Response Methods and Properties

Most of the methods and properties outlined in Table 6-1 are convenient alternatives to the methods covered already in the book. In other words, we can accomplish most of the logic with the main methods, but knowing the following shortcuts can save developers a few keystrokes and improve readability. For example, `response.type()` is a niche case of `response.header()` for a Content-Type only header.

Table 6-1. Method and property alternatives

Method/Property	Description/Conditions	API
`response.get()`	String value of response header for a passed header type	http://expressjs.com/api.html#res.get
`response.cookie()`	Takes cookie key/value pair and sets it on response	http://expressjs.com/api.html#res.cookie
`response.clearCookie()`	Takes cookie key/name and optional path parameter to clear the cookies	http://expressjs.com/api.html#res.clearCookie
`response.location()`	Takes a relative, absolute, or full path as a string and sets that value to Location response header	http://expressjs.com/api.html#res.location
`response.charset`	The charset value of the response	http://expressjs.com/api.html#res.charset
`response.type()`	Takes a string and sets it as a value of Content-Type header	http://expressjs.com/api.html#res.type
`response.format()`	Takes an object as a mapping of types and responses and executes them according to Accepted request header	http://expressjs.com/api.html#res.format
`response.attachment()`	Takes optional file name as a string and sets Content-Disposition (and if file name provided, Content-Type) header(s) to attachment and file type accordingly	http://expressjs.com/api.html#res.attachment
`response.sendfile()`	Takes path to a file on the server and various options and callback parameters, and sends the file to the requester	http://expressjs.com/api.html#res.sendfile
`response.download()`	Takes same parameters as `response.sendfile()`, and sets Content-Disposition and calls `response.sendfile()`	http://expressjs.com/api.html#res.download
`response.links()`	Takes an object of URLs to populate Links response header	http://expressjs.com/api.html#res.links

You can find the full source code for this chapter's example in the ch6 folder and on GitHub (https://github.com/azat-co/expressapiref/tree/master/ch6). Listing 6-1 shows what the ch6/app.js file looks like (including other examples).

Listing 6-1. ch6/app.js File

```javascript
var express = require('express');
var fs = require('fs');
var path = require('path');
var favicon = require('serve-favicon');
var logger = require('morgan');
var cookieParser = require('cookie-parser');
var bodyParser = require('body-parser');

var routes = require('./routes/index');

var largeImagePath = path.join(__dirname, 'files', 'large-image.jpg');

var app = express();

// View engine setup
app.set('views', path.join(__dirname, 'views'));
app.set('view engine', 'jade');
app.use(logger('combined'));
app.use(favicon(path.join(__dirname, 'public', 'favicon.ico')));
app.use(bodyParser.json());
app.use(bodyParser.urlencoded({extended: true}));
app.use(cookieParser('abc'));
app.use(express.static(path.join(__dirname, 'public')));

app.use('/', routes);

app.get('/render', function(req, res) {
  res.render('render');
});

app.get('/render-title', function(req, res) {
  res.render('index', {title: 'Pro Express.js'});
});
```

```
app.get('/locals', function(req, res){
  res.locals = { title: 'Pro Express.js' };
  res.render('index');
});

app.get('/set-html', function(req, res) {
  // Some code
  res.set('Content-Type', 'text/html');
  res.end('<html><body>' +
    '<h1>Express.js Guide</h1>' +
    '</body></html>');
});

app.get('/set-csv', function(req, res) {
  var body = 'title, tags\n' +
    'Practical Node.js, node.js express.js\n' +
    'Rapid Prototyping with JS, backbone.js node.js mongodb\n' +
    'JavaScript: The Good Parts, javascript\n';
  res.set({'Content-Type': 'text/csv',
    'Content-Length': body.length,
    'Set-Cookie': ['type=reader', 'language=javascript']});
  res.end(body);
});

app.get('/status', function(req, res) {
  res.status(200).end();
});

app.get('/send-ok', function(req, res) {
  res.status(200).send({message: 'Data was submitted successfully.'});
});

app.get('/send-err', function(req, res) {
  res.status(500).send({message: 'Oops, the server is down.'});
});

app.get('/send-buf', function(req, res) {
  res.set('Content-Type', 'text/plain');
  res.status(200).send(new Buffer('text data that will be converted into
Buffer'));
});

app.get('/json', function(req, res) {
  res.status(200).json([{title: 'Practical Node.js', tags: 'node.js express.js'},
    {title: 'Rapid Prototyping with JS', tags: 'backbone.js node.js mongodb'},
    {title: 'JavaScript: The Good Parts', tags: 'javascript'}
  ]);
});
```

```
app.get('/non-stream', function(req, res) {
  var file = fs.readFileSync(largeImagePath);
  res.end(file);
});

app.get('/non-stream2', function(req, res) {
  var file = fs.readFile(largeImagePath, function(error, data){
    res.end(data);
  });
});

app.get('/stream1', function(req, res) {
  var stream = fs.createReadStream(largeImagePath);
  stream.pipe(res);
});

app.get('/stream2', function(req, res) {
  var stream = fs.createReadStream(largeImagePath);
  stream.on('data', function(data) {
    res.write(data);
  });
  stream.on('end', function() {
    res.end();
  });
});

/// Catch 404 and forward to error handler
app.use(function(req, res, next) {
    var err = new Error('Not Found');
    err.status = 404;
    next(err);
});

/// Error handlers

// Development error handler
// Will print stacktrace
if (app.get('env') === 'development') {
    app.use(function(err, req, res, next) {
        res.status(err.status || 500);
        res.render('error', {
            message: err.message,
            error: err
        });
    });
}
```

```
// Production error handler
// No stacktraces leaked to user
app.use(function(err, req, res, next) {
    res.status(err.status || 500);
    res.render('error', {
        message: err.message,
        error: {}
    });
});

module.exports = app;

var debug = require('debug')('request');

app.set('port', process.env.PORT || 3000);

var server = app.listen(app.get('port'), function() {
  debug('Express server listening on port ' + server.address().port);
});
```

Streams

As far as sending nonstreaming responses between response.send() and response.
end(), you should be well covered from the previous discussion. However, for streaming
data back, response.send() is not going to work; instead, you should use the response
object (which is a writable stream and inherited from http.ServerResponse):

```
app.get('/stream1', function(req, res) {
  var stream = fs.createReadStream(largeImagePath);
  stream.pipe(res);
});
```

Alternatively, use event handlers with data and end events:

```
app.get('/stream2', function(req, res) {
  var stream = fs.createReadStream(largeImagePath);
  stream.on('data', function(data) {
    res.write(data);
  });
  stream.on('end', function() {
    res.end();
  });
});
```

The nonstreaming equivalent might look like this:

```
app.get('/non-stream', function(req, res) {
  var file = fs.readFileSync(largeImagePath);
  res.end(file);
});
```

For this demo we're using a relatively large image of 5.1MB, which is located at ch6/files/large-image.jpg. Notice the drastic difference in waiting time between streaming, shown in Figure 6-12, and nonstreaming, shown in Figure 6-13. The nonstreaming route waited for the whole file to load and then sent the whole file back (~49ms), while the streaming route waited much less (only ~7ms). The fact that we use a synchronous function in the nonstreaming example shouldn't matter because we load pages serially (one by one).

Figure 6-12. Streaming an image shows a faster waiting time than nonstreaming

119

Figure 6-13. *Nonstreaming an image shows a slower waiting time than streaming*

■ **Tip**   In addition to using streams for response, streams can be use for requests as well. Streaming is useful when dealing with large amounts of data (video, binary data, audio, etc.) because the streams allow processing to start without finishing transfers. For more information about streams, check out `https://github.com/substack/stream-handbook` and `https://github.com/substack/stream-adventure`.

Summary

If you've made it thus far through each of the properties of the response, you probably know more than an average Express.js developer. Congratulations! Understanding request and response is the bread and butter (or meat and veggies for paleo lifestyle people) of the Express.js development.

We're almost done with the Express.js interface (a.k.a. API). The remaining pieces are error handling and actually starting the app.

CHAPTER 7

■ ■ ■

Error Handling and Running an App

Good web applications must have informative error messages to notify clients exactly why their request has failed. Errors might be caused either by the client (e.g., wrong input data) or by the server (e.g., a bug in the code).

The client might be a browser, in which case the application should display an HTML page. For example, a 404 page should display when the requested resource is not found. Or the client might be another application consuming our resources via the REST API. In this case, the application should send the appropriate HTTP status code and the message in the JSON format (or XML or another format that is supported). For these reasons, it's always the best practice to customize error-handling code when developing a serious application.

In a typical Express.js application, error handlers follow the routes. Error handling deserves its own section of the book because it's different from other middleware. After the error handlers, we'll cover the Express.js application methods and ways to start the Express.js app. Therefore, the major topics of this chapter are as follows:

- Error handling
- Running an app

Error Handling

Because of the asynchronous nature of Node.js and callback patterns, it's not a trivial task to catch and log for future analysis the state in which errors happen. The use of domains for error handling in Express.js is a more advanced technique and, for most implementations right out of the box, framework's built-in error handling might prove sufficient (along with custom error handling middleware).

We can start with the basic development error handler from our cli-app example (https://github.com/azat-co/expressapiref/tree/master/cli-app). The error handler spits out the error status (500, Internal Server Error), stack trace, and error message. It is enabled by this code *only* when the app is in development mode:

```
if (app.get('env') === 'development') {
    app.use(function(err, req, res, next) {
        res.status(err.status || 500);
        res.render('error', {
            message: err.message,
            error: err
        });
    });
}
```

■ **Tip** app.get('env') is a convenient method for process.env.NODE_ENV; in other words, the preceding line can be rewritten with process.env.NODE_ENV === 'development'.

This makes sense because error handling is typically used across the whole application. Therefore, it's best to implement it as middleware.

For custom error-handler implementations, the middleware is the same as any other except that it has one more parameter, error (or err for short):

```
// Main middleware
app.use(function(err, req, res, next) {
  // Do logging and user-friendly error message display
  console.error(err);
  res.status(500).send();
});
// Routes
```

We can use res.status(500).end() to achieve a similar result, because we're not sending any data (e.g., an error message). It's recommended to send at least a brief error message, because it will help the debugging process when problems occur. In fact, the response can be anything: JSON, text, a redirect to a static page, or something else.

For most front-end and other JSON clients, the preferred format is, of course, JSON:

```
app.use(function(err, req, res, next) {
  // Do logging and user-friendly error message display
  console.error(err);
  res.status(500).send({status:500, message: 'internal error',
type:'internal'});
})
```

■ **Note**   Developers can use the `req.xhr` property or check if the `Accept` request header
has the `application/json` value.

The most straightforward way is to just send a text:

```
app.use(function(err, req, res, next) {
  // Do logging and user-friendly error message display
  console.error(err);
  res.status(500).send('internal server error');
})
```

Or, if we know that it's secure to output the error message, we could use the following:

```
app.use(function(err, req, res, next) {
  // Do logging and user-friendly error message display
  console.error(err);
  res.status(500).send('internal server error: ' + err);
})
```

To simply render a static error page with the name 500 (template is the file 500.jade,
the engine is Jade) and the default extension, we could use

```
app.use(function(err, req, res, next) {
  // Do logging and user-friendly error message display
  console.error(err);
  // Assuming that template engine is plugged in
  res.render('500');
})
```

Or we could use the following, if we want to overwrite the file extension, for a full
filename of 500.html:

```
app.use(function(err, req, res, next) {
  // Do logging and user-friendly error message display
  console.error(err);
  // Assuming that template engine is plugged in
  res.render('500.html');
})
```

We can also use res.redirect():

```
app.use(function(err, req, res, next) {
  // Do logging and user-friendly error message display
  res.redirect('/public/500.html');
})
```

Always using proper HTTP response statuses such as 401, 400, 500, and so on, is recommended. Refer to Table 7-1 for a quick reference.

Table 7-1. *Main HTTP Status Codes*

Code	Name	Meaning
200	OK	Standard response for successful HTTP requests
201	Created	Request has been fulfilled. New resource created
204	No Content	Request processed. No content returned
301	Moved Permanently	This and all future requests directed to the given URI
304	Not Modified	Resource has not been modified since last requested
400	Bad Request	Request cannot be fulfilled due to bad syntax
401	Unauthorized	Authentication is possible, but has failed
403	Forbidden	Server refuses to respond to request
404	Not Found	Requested resource could not be found
500	Internal Server Error	Generic error message when server fails
501	Not Implemented	Server does not recognize method or lacks ability to fulfill
503	Service Unavailable	Server is currently unavailable

■ **Tip** For the complete list of available HTTP methods, please refer to RFC 2616 at www.w3.org/Protocols/rfc2616/rfc2616-sec10.html.

This is how we can send the status 500 (Internal Server Error) without sending back any data:

```
app.use(function(err, req, res, next) {
  // Do logging and user-friendly error message display
  res.end(500);
})
```

To trigger an error from within our request handlers and middleware, we can just call

```
app.get('/', function(req, res, next){
  next(error);
});
```

Or, if we want to pass a specific error message, then we create an Error object and pass it to next():

```
app.get('/', function(req,res,next){
  next(new Error('Something went wrong :-('));
});
```

It would be a good idea to use the return keyword for processing multiple error-prone cases and combine both of the previous approaches. For example, we pass the database error to next(), but an empty query result will not cause a database error (i.e., error will be null), so we check for this condition with !users:

```
// A GET route for the user entity
app.get('/users', function(req, res, next) {
  // A database query that will get us any users from the collection
  db.get('users').find({}, function(error, users) {
    if (error) return next(error);
    if (!users) return next(new Error('No users found.'));
    // Do something, if fail the return next(error);
    res.send(users);
});
```

For complex apps, it's best to use multiple error handlers. For example, use one for XHR/AJAX requests, one for normal requests, and one for generic catch-everything-else. It's also a good idea to use named functions (and organize them in modules) instead of anonymous ones.

■ **Tip** There's an easy way out in regards to managing error handling that is especially good for development purposes. It's called errorhandler (https://www.npmjs.org/package/errorhandler) and it has the default error handlers for Express.js/Connect.js. For more information on errorhandler, refer to the Chapter 2.

Running an App

The Express.js class provides a few *app-wide* objects and methods on its object, which is app in our examples. These objects and methods are recommended because they can improve code reuse and maintenance. For example, instead of hard-coding the number 3000 everywhere, we can just assign it once with app.set('PORT', 3000);. Then, if we need to update it later, we have only one place where it needs to be changed. Therefore, we'll cover the following properties and methods in this section:

app.locals

app.render()

app.mountpath

```
app.on('mount', callback)

app.path()

app.listen()
```

The source code for this example is in the ch7 and https://github.com/azat-co/
expressapiref/tree/master/ch7.

app.locals

The app.locals object is similar to the res.locals object (discussed in Chapter 6) in the
sense that it exposes data to templates. However, there's a main difference: app.locals
makes its properties available in *all* templates rendered by app, while res.locals restricts
them *only* to that request. Therefore, developers need to be careful not to reveal any
sensitive information via app.locals. The best use case for this is app-wide settings such
as locations, URLs, contact info, and so forth. For example:

```
app.locals.lang = 'en';
app.locals.appName = 'HackHall';
```

The app.locals object can also be invoked like a function:

```
app.locals([
  author: 'Azat Mardan',
  email: 'hi@azat.co',
  website: 'http://proexpressjs.com'
]);
```

app.render( )

The app.render() method is invoked either with a view name and a callback or with a
view name, data, and a callback. For example, the system might have an e-mail template
for a "Thank you for signing up" message and another for "Reset your password:"

```
var sendgrid  = require('sendgrid')(api_user, api_key);

var sendThankYouEmail = function (userEmail) {
  app.render('emails/thank-you', function (err, html){
    if (err) return console.error(err);
    sendgrid.send({
      to:       userEmail,
      from:     app.get('appEmail'),
      subject:  'Thank you for signing up',
      html:  html // The html value is returned by the app.render
    }, function(err, json) {
```

```
      if (err) { return console.error(err); }
      console.log(json);
    });
  });
};

var resetPasswordEmail = function(userEmail) {
  app.render('emails/reset-password', {token: generateResetToken()},
function(err, html){
    if (err) return console.error(err);
    sendgrid.send({
      to:       userEmail,
      from:     app.get('appEmail'),
      subject:  'Reset your password',
      html:     html
    }, function(err, json) {
      if (err) { return console.error(err); }
      console.log(json);
    });
  });
};
```

■ **Note**   The sendgrid module used in the example is available at NPM[1] and GitHub.[2]

---

app.mountpath

The app.mountpath property is used in the mounted/sub apps. Mounted apps are sub-apps that can be used for better code reuse and organization. The app.mountpath property returns the path on which app is mounted.

For example, in ch7/app-mountpath.js there are two sub applications: post and comment. The post is mounted on the /post path of app, while comment is mounted on /comment of post. As a result of logs, mountpath returns values /post and /comment:

```
var express= require('express'),
  app = express(),
  post = express(),
  comment = express();

app.use('/post', post);
post.use('/comment', comment);
```

---

[1]https://www.npmjs.org/package/sendgrid
[2]https://github.com/sendgrid/sendgrid-nodejs

```
console.log(app.mountpath); // ''
console.log(post.mountpath); // '/post'
console.log(comment.mountpath); // '/comment'
```

app.on('mount', function(parent){...})

The mount is triggered when the sub app is mounted on a specific path of a parent/main app. For example, in ch7/app-on-mount.js, we have two sub apps with on mount event listeners that print parents' mountpaths. The values of the paths are / for post's parent (app) and /post for comment's parent (post):

```
var express= require('express'),
  app = express(),
  post = express(),
  comment = express();

post.on('mount', function(parent){
  console.log(parent.mountpath); // '/'
})
comment.on('mount', function(parent){
  console.log(parent.mountpath); // '/post'
})

app.use('/post', post);
post.use('/comment', comment);
```

app.path( )

The app.path() method will return the canonical path for the Express.js application. This is useful if you are using multiple Express.js apps mounted to different routes (for better code organization).

For example, you have comments resource (routes related to comments) for posts by the way of mounting the comment app on the /comment path of the post app. But you can still get the "full" path with comment.path() (from ch7/app-path.js):

```
var express= require('express'),
  app = express(),
  post = express(),
  comment = express();

app.use('/post', post);
post.use('/comment', comment);
```

```
console.log(app.path());    // ''
console.log(post.path());   // '/post'
console.log(comment.path()); // '/post/comment'
```

app.listen( )

The Express.js app.listen(port, [hostname,] [backlog,] [callback]) method is akin to server.listen()[3] from the core Node.js http module. This method is one of the ways to start an Express.js app. The port is a port number on which the server should accept incoming requests. The hostname is the name of the domain. You might need to set it when you deploy your apps to the cloud. The backlog is the maximum number of queued pending connections. The default is 511. And the callback is an asynchronous function that is called when the server is booted.

To spin up the Express.js app directly on a particular port (3000):

```
var express = require('express');
var app = express();
// ... Configuration
// ... Routes
app.listen(3000);
```

This approach is used by Express.js Generator. In it, the app.js file doesn't start a server, but it exports the object with

```
module.exports = app;
```

We don't run the app.js file with $ node app.js either. Instead, we launch a shell script www with $ ./bin/www. The shell script has this special string on its first line:

```
#!/usr/bin/env node
```

The line above turns the shell script into a Node.js program. This program imports the app object from the app.js file, sets the port, and starts the app server with listen() and a callback:

```
var debug = require('debug')('cli-app');
var app = require('../app');

app.set('port', process.env.PORT || 3000);

var server = app.listen(app.get('port'), function() {
  debug('Express server listening on port ' + server.address().port);
});
```

---

[3]http://nodejs.org/api/http.html#http_server_listen_port_hostname_backlog_callback

Having your server object exported as a module is necessary when another process requires the object, e.g., a testing framework. In the previous example, the main server file (cli-app/app.js) exported the object and there is was no way of starting the server with $ node app. If you don't want to have a separate shell file for launching the server, but still want to export the server when you need to, you can use the following trick. The gist of this approach is to check whether the module is a dependency with require.main === module condition. If it's true, then we start the application. If it's not, then we expose the methods and the app object.

```
var server = http.createServer(app);
var boot = function () {
  server.listen(app.get('port'), function(){
    console.info('Express server listening on port ' + app.get('port'));
  });
}
var shutdown = function() {
  server.close();
}
if (require.main === module) {
  boot();
} else {
  console.info('Running app as a module');
  exports.boot = boot;
  exports.shutdown = shutdown;
  exports.port = app.get('port');
}
```

Another way to start a server besides app.listen() is to apply the Express.js app to the core Node.js server function. This is useful for spawning an HTTP server and an HTTPS server with the same code base:

```
var express = require('express');
var https = require('https');
var http = require('http');
var app = express();
var ops = require('conf/ops');
//... Configuration
//... Routes
http.createServer(app).listen(80);
https.createServer(ops, app).listen(443);
```

You can create a self-signed SSL certificate (for example, the server.crt file) to test your HTTPS server locally for development purposes with OpenSSL by running these commands:

```
$ sudo ssh-keygen -f host.key
$ sudo openssl req -new -key host.key -out request.csr
$ sudo openssl x509 -req -days 365 -in request.csr -signkey host.key -out
  server.crt
```

The OpenSSL is an open-source implementation of Secure Socket Layer (SSL) protocol and a toolkit. You can find more about it at https://www.openssl.org. When you use OpenSSL, Chrome and many other browsers will complain with a warning about self-signed certificates—you can ignore it by clicking Proceed anyway (see Figure 7-1).

Figure 7-1. *You can ignore this warning cause by a self-signed SSL certificate*

■ **Tip** To install OpenSSL on Mac OS X, run $ brew install OpenSSL. On Windows, download the installer from http://gnuwin32.sourceforge.net/packages/openssl.htm. On Ubuntu, run apt-get install OpenSSL.

After server.crt is ready, feed it to the https.createServer() methods like this (the ch7/app.js file):

```
var express = require('express');
var https = require('https');
var http = require('http');
var app = express();
var fs = require('fs');
```

```
var ops = {
    key: fs.readFileSync('host.key'),
    cert: fs.readFileSync('server.crt') ,
    passphrase: 'your_secret_passphrase'
};

app.get('/', function(request, response){
  response.send('ok');
});
http.createServer(app).listen(80);
https.createServer(ops, app).listen(443);
```

The passphrase is the one you used during the certificate creation with OpenSSL. Leave it out if you didn't put in any passphrase. To start the process, you might have to use sudo, such as $ sudo node app.

If everything worked well, you should see an okay message as shown in Figure 7-2.

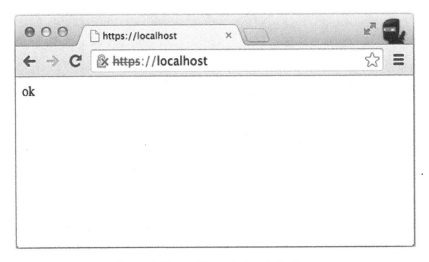

Figure 7-2. *Using self-signed SSL certificate for local development*

Finally, if your application performs a lot of blocking work, you might want to start multiple processes with cluster module.

Summary

This chapter covered multiple ways to implement error handlers, the app object interface, and ways to start the Express.js server. This concludes Express.js Deep API Reference. Hopefully, you've learned many new properties and methods of the Express. js framework's objects, such as response, request, and the app itself. If you had any doubts about middleware, then Chapter 2 cleared any concerns. Last but not least, we covered routing, error handling and template utilization topics. All these topics built your foundation so you can apply this knowledge to creating amazing and exciting new apps with Express.js.

If you like this reference book but wish for more more practical and complex topics, which include "how to use X" or "how to do Y" examples. I highly recommend you to read the Pro Express.js and Practical Node.js books from Apress and me.

Index